HODDER AND STOUGHTON'S
PEOPLE'S LIBRARY

General Editor : Sidney Dark

JESUS CHRIST

BY

ANTHONY C. DEANE, M.A.

HODDER AND STOUGHTON

PUBLISHERS   LONDON

First Published . . . Oct. 1927
Reprinted . . . . . Dec. 1927
Reprinted . . . . . Nov. 1930

Printed in Great Britain for Hodder and Stoughton, Limited,
by Richard Clay & Sons, Limited, Bungay, Suffolk.

PREFACE

I WANT to make clear, if I can, the special scope and aim of this book.

It is not, in the usual sense, a "Life of Christ"—a work, that is, which re-tells the whole story of the Gospels, weaving the narratives of the four Evangelists into one, describing every incident, re-interpreting each parable. Of such books some new and valuable examples have been published within recent years, and I have not tried to compete with them.

Yet their copiousness sometimes discomfits readers who turn to them with a special need; people (and my work brings me into touch with many of them) who feel themselves confronted afresh by that enduring question, "Whom say ye that I am?" And there are others, who having answered, would like to be more sure that the answer

they gave was justified. They find that
the " Lives of Christ " are largely taken up
with historical and geographical detail,
with picturesque descriptions of buildings
and scenery, with erudite doctrinal or
critical discussions, even with the writer's
own moralizings—with, in short, subsidiary
matter which, though of much interest in
itself, does not help those whose need is like
that of the Greeks in Jerusalem :—" Sir,
we would see Jesus." It may be said that
such people must be referred to the Gospels.
That is obviously true. Yet the Gospels
themselves presuppose for their right understanding certain knowledge which their
first readers had, which modern study has
recaptured, but which as yet is not often in
the possession of the general reader.

What, then, I have tried—how imperfectly !—to do, is not to supply an answer
to our Lord's supreme question, but to
place before the reader the material on
which an answer can be based. His it must
be ; each of us must frame his own reply.

Yet a concise statement of the evidence may help him in framing it. If we are rightly to appraise the claims of Jesus, we must know something of the age and its religious thought in which his work was done. We must see how he appeared to his contemporaries, how he conceived his mission, by what means he set himself to fulfil it. We must see not only how he lived, but how he died, and triumphed over death.

That is the kind of evidence I have attempted to place clearly before the reader. In such an attempt it is essential not to obscure the main facts by a mass of detail. Necessarily, therefore, I have omitted much that is recorded in the Gospels, the better to concentrate on the chief characteristics of our Lord's ministry and the great turning-points in his earthly life. To the fact that the book is written with this special aim, and to its limitations of space, I hope the reader will ascribe omissions that else might seem unpardonable.

A word should be added about two small

details. I have followed the usage of the
English Bible—both in the Authorized and
Revised Versions—by not employing capital
letters for pronouns referring to our Lord.
Otherwise, in a book wholly about him,
each page is overloaded with capitals, and
takes on an unreal, artificial look, which
somewhat repels the reader. After all,
the designers of our English Bible are an
authority good enough to follow.

Also it will be observed that, generally
speaking, I have described our Lord by his
human name. To do otherwise would seem
to prejudge the issue on which, as I have
insisted, each of us must form his own
decision. " Jesus " implies a question :
" Christ " supplies the answer. It is the
one adequate answer. But I want the
reader to reach that conclusion for
himself.

Let my last personal word be one of
profound thankfulness to God for all that
the writing of this little book, despite its
faults, has taught me. . . . There shall be

no " I " within the book itself ! Its aim
will be fulfilled indeed if it can help forward
any reader until, book and writer alike
forgotten, he stands face to face with Jesus
Christ.   A. C. D.

CONTENTS

CHAPTER I

THE PROLOGUE

I

In the year 26 A.D. southern Palestine, an outlying part of the Roman Empire, was stirred as it had not been for upwards of four centuries. True, in that long period its inhabitants had undergone many vicissitudes. The ancient race of Israel had passed in turn under the sway of many rulers. Rome was the latest of them, but Rome itself could not enforce tranquillity upon a people who claimed to be the elect of God and exempt from all earthly dominion. Of tumults and disturbances there had been many. They had been particularly frequent within the last thirty years—years during which the son of a woman of Nazareth had grown to manhood. National feeling had compelled changes in the system of local government administered from Rome. Political intrigues had been planned and put down. Religious fanatics had tried, with varying degrees of brief success, to stir revolt. At length had come an interlude of outward calm. But it was the calm of embittered despair rather than of acquiescence. Any moment might bring news of some fresh local insurrection. Such news had become almost commonplace. It would cause little hope in Jerusalem, and little harm at Rome.

The news that came, however, was vastly more significant and unexpected. It was news of a religious revival. It was news without parallel for centuries. It agitated, though in very different fashions, priests in the Temple and peasants in the villages. It was the theme of eager talk in market-place and synagogue. A teacher had come, report declared, who again spoke " in the name of the Lord." Once more God had visited His people. Once more there was a prophet in Israel.

The prophet was John the Baptist. The excitement stirred by his coming outdid any that news of battle or revolution could have provoked. Apart from the power of his preaching, apart from the success of his crusade, the mere fact that here was one who dared to teach as a prophet astounded Palestine. The news ran through the land like fire.

II

To understand this feeling, we must have in mind the religious history of the nation.

Over a long period two rival strains of doctrine had struggled for mastery. The one derived its strength from the priests, the other from the prophets. The priests encouraged the idea—natural enough in a race conscious of a religion nobler and purer than those of surrounding nations—that God could have no regard for any but the Jews. From the right doctrine that Jehovah alone was their God grew the wrong doctrine that Jehovah was their God alone. With Israel only He had a covenant, and this covenant was embodied in the Law. Therefore the Law was all-important. The one virtue required of man was "righteousness," and righteousness began and ended, so the doctrine of the priests affirmed, in a precise observance of the letter of the Law.

The Temple, with its Holy of Holies and its code of sacrifices, strengthened this idea of a local and legal Deity; the loss of the Temple during the period of the Captivity weakened it. This enabled a new and nobler view of religion to be put forward by the Prophets. They affirmed that God had a care for the Gentiles, and not for the Jews alone. They taught that true "righteousness" lay, not in the offering of sacrifices and mechanical obedience to the Law, but in uprightness of character, in purity of life, and in a will set to obey God. Their message was nobly summarized by Micah: "Shall I come before God with burnt offerings? Will the Lord be pleased with thousands of rams, or ten thousand rivers of oil? He hath shewed thee, O man, what is good; and what doth the Lord require of thee but to do justly, and to love mercy, and to walk humbly with thy God? "

This prophetic doctrine, with its liberalism of outlook, its view of religion as a personal relationship with God, made a profound impression. For a time it overcame the sterile creed of legalism. But the re-building of the Temple after the Captivity restored the dominance of the priests. They fought against the influence of the prophets, and ultimately they prevailed. Prophecy was silenced. The prophetic writings already extant were to be understood only as the priests chose to interpret them. Further prophecy was forbidden. Through four-and-a-half centuries no writer dared to give religious teaching in his own name. New religious books had to be put forward under the names of great men of the past, and were given such titles as " The Assumption of Moses," " The Testaments of the

B

Twelve Patriarchs," "The Ascension of Isaiah." This literature, known as "Apocalyptic," was continued into New Testament times. It strove to hearten the Jews through ages of adversity by encouraging them to expect some great manifestation of God, when He would overthrow their enemies and establish a visible sovereignty among His chosen people. Thus the influence of Apocalyptic was to make devout Jews look forward to a triumphant coming of God's kingdom and the ending of alien rule. It linked their religious hopes with their political aspirations.

Yet Apocalyptic could not take the place of the prophetic teaching. It appealed to the imagination rather than to the conscience. Legalism tightened its grip as the official religion of Israel. As time went on, it was divided into two schools, under rival sets of leaders. In Jerusalem were the Sadducees; a small, aristocratic, and wealthy body of politicians. On matters of religion their attitude was one of extreme conservatism. Thus they, unlike all other Jews, rejected belief in the doctrine of angels, spirits, and immortality, on the ground that they could find no support for it in the Mosaic Law. They upheld the Law, and the Law alone.

Outside Jerusalem the direct power of the Sadducees was small. Elsewhere the religious leaders were the rival sect of the Pharisees, whose rabbis taught in most of the provincial synagogues. While the Sadducees adhered to the strict letter of the original Law, the Pharisees upheld it as expanded and interpreted by " tradition." In fact, with them the written and oral " traditions of the elders " were supreme. Their code regulated every moment of life, from birth to burial. The Jew found his most commonplace acts set about by ceremonies, and the ways in which he was to rise, wash, eat, work, clothe himself, and pray were all minutely prescribed for him. Exact observance of these multitudinous rules constituted " righteousness," and the whole of righteousness. Honour, kindness, and morality might be disregarded if some method could be found of circumventing, without technical infringement, the precepts which enjoined them. Any dubious point must be referred to a rabbi; none but the authorized rabbis were permitted to expound the Law, or to set forth the tradition which interpreted it.

In practice this code was a burden too heavy to be borne. Ordinary people could not escape frequent transgressions of it. Yet to violate it in any detail, even unintentionally, was to be unrighteous, and to incur the wrath of God. No wonder that eager souls yearned for teaching such as the prophets had given to bygone generations; teaching which brought the individual into touch with God, and set right conduct and desires above ceremonial observance. It seemed vain, after four-and-a-half centuries of silence, to expect a prophet's voice. Yet there was a gleam of hope in the remembrance that the latest of the prophets had predicted the reappearance of Elijah before the day of the Lord should come.

III

Such, then, was the condition of Palestine in the year 26. It was an age of spiritual hunger and of political discontent. Its prevailing restlessness was increased by economic pressure. Under the old theocratic conception, taxes and dues were levied for religious purposes only. They had grown heavier with the increasing power of the priests, bent upon maintaining the Temple in splendour and themselves in opulence. But of this existing religious taxation the Romans took no account when they exacted tribute from Palestine, as from the other provinces of their Empire. Thus every Jew was doubly burdened, for civil and religious purposes. He had to supply both the Temple tax and Cæsar's tribute. This resulted in poverty and heightened discontent. Political upheaval or social revolt would have been welcomed by multitudes. But blended with, and strengthening, all such desires was religious dissatisfaction. It could not be, surely, that God had forsaken His people. It could not be that He would suffer them indefinitely to bear the yoke of a heathen power, to remain despised and poverty-stricken. It could not be the final form of religion, this hopeless attempt to comply with an impossible code, this system of a wealthy and complacent priesthood, of rabbis revelling in casuistry that never touched the conscience, that never filled the hungry soul. There would be, there must be, a change. Prophecy and Apocalyptic alike · had encouraged them to expect that Jehovah would manifest Himself, and send deliverance, and establish His kingdom. Yet the years passed on, and what sign was there of fulfilment? Where was the national leader, or the great social reformer, whom they could follow? Where was the promised Messiah; where the

prophet who was to be the Messiah's
herald? In restless discontent, political,
social, and religious; in hope that despaired
and despair that yet hoped, the inhabitants
of Palestine passed their days.

And then John the Baptist came.

Having in mind the facts we have
summarized, can we wonder at the immense
excitement caused by his coming? "All
men reasoned in their hearts concerning
John." Report said that he declared the
Kingdom of God to be at hand. Could this
indeed be—the Christ? Others brought
news of his manner of life. He had dwelt
in the wilderness; he wore, like Elijah, a
garment of camel's hair and a leathern
girdle, he was an ascetic—this, they said,
must be Elijah reincarnate, sent as Malachi
had foretold. At least he must be a
prophet, for he was no Pharisee or Sadducee.
In defiance of their prohibitions, he was
teaching as the prophets of old had done.
And so, full of eager talk, and wonder, and
various surmises, the people streamed forth

to hear him for themselves. From town
and village they came; " there went out
unto him all the country of Judæa and all
they of Jerusalem," to be joined presently
by travellers from the northern territory of
Galilee.

Their questions were promptly given
explicit answers. John would have no
misunderstanding about himself or his work.
He was not, he said, the Christ. He was
preparing the way for one greater than
himself. He was not the leader of a social
or political revolution, as many hoped.
" What shall we do? " asked the most
impoverished of his hearers, ready enough
for pillage if he gave the word. But the
answer was that the poor man should share
the little he had with him who was even
poorer. " What shall we do? " asked the
publicans, Jews employed to collect the
Roman tribute. It was a crucial question,
like " Is it lawful to give tribute to Cæsar? "
Perhaps the answer expected was : " You
must abandon your calling. You must

cease to collect these enforced payments from your countrymen to an alien power, against which I shall encourage them to rise." But John's reply showed that he would lead no political movement, as his first answer had shown he would lead no social revolution. The publicans were merely warned not to exact more than was legally due. " And what shall we do ? " asked the soldiers " on duty "—such is the force of the Greek word. They were Jewish soldiers employed probably, as we should say, on police duty. They too received no encouragement to desert or rebel. They were to levy no blackmail, and to be content with their pay. John's replies made it clear that he had not come to encourage any movement of class warfare, or any political insurrection against Rome.

His real message was comprised in the one word—Repent. He awoke dormant consciences. He stirred the sense of sin. He made men and women realize the worthlessness of that merely external " righteous-

ness " which their official teachers upheld.
Like the older prophets, he insisted on the
need of clean hands and a pure heart.
More boldly even than the older prophets,
he swept away the complacency of those
who imagined all must be well with them
in God's sight, whatever their conduct,
since they belonged to His chosen race.
" Think not to say within yourselves, We
have Abraham to our father; for I say
unto you that God is able of these stones
to raise up children unto Abraham." They
must bring forth " fruits meet for repentance," the fruits of a pure life. And through
all this teaching sounded the note of extreme
urgency; the time was short, the axe was
already near the root of the tree; the
kingdom of God was at hand !

Huge crowds heard, and trembled, and
rejoiced, and were convinced. They owned
their wrongdoings. They pledged themselves to nobler ways of life. Then, as an
outward sign of repentance, they were
baptized by John; they submitted to that

rite of cleansing which was widely known, and shared by many forms of religion. It was amazing to see those multitudes, of all classes, hastening to the banks of the Jordan. It was a time of vast significance in the history of Israel. It was the reinstatement of prophecy after a break of four-and-a-half centuries. It was one of the greatest spiritual revivals the world has known.

We are not to suppose that John baptized all who came indiscriminately, without question. The narrative makes it clear that he did not. When "many of the Pharisees and Sadducees" came, he discerned their motive, which was simply to find grounds for setting on foot proceedings against him. He met them with grim invective, and sent them away. The people whom he baptized must "confess their sins," must show themselves in private talk to be really penitent, before their baptism. Then, full of new hopes for themselves, and with an eager looking for the promised

Kingdom of God, they returned. And all men, having heard his teaching about righteousness, so akin to that of the bygone prophets, so unlike the narrow legalistic conception of the rabbis, acknowledged John to be a prophet indeed.

IV

One day among the travellers from Galilee who came to him was a carpenter of Nazareth, named Jesus.

He asked John to baptize him. But as they spoke together apart, John felt a strange sense of awe, recognized that here was a character the purity of which put his own to shame, and made him keenly conscious of his imperfections. " I have need to be baptized of thee," he remonstrated, " and comest thou to me? " But Jesus was insistent, " for thus it becometh us to fulfil all righteousness," he said. The task which he and the Baptist would share—a task on which the Baptist already had been busy—was to rescue " righteousness " from

the narrow interpretation fastened upon it
by legalism, and to " fulfil " it ; to fill it full
of new and true meaning.   As a prelude to
the accomplishing of that work, baptism
was for Jesus an act, not of purification, but
of consecration. He was baptized, and
as he stepped out of the water, he saw the
heavens open, and the Spirit of God
descending as a dove, and heard a voice :
" Thou art my beloved Son, in thee I am
well pleased."   The earliest of the Gospels
(St. Mark's) makes it clear that the vision
was seen, and the voice heard, by Jesus only.
It must have been he who described it to
John, and afterwards to his disciples, as he
told them also of his temptations.

We will not involve ourselves here with
questions which must needs be profoundly
mysterious, and indeed unanswerable.   We
will not discuss the relationship between the
divine and the human in the nature of Jesus
Christ.   So far as, in deep reverence, we can
even venture our imperfect surmises, we
shall be better equipped for such thinking

when we have completed our study of the life. Indeed, at the outset we shall do well to emphasize a truth that seems often to be forgotten. That fact is the cumulative character of the evidence for the claims of Jesus. People are far too apt to consider in isolation some one incident, or saying, or narrative. No limited scrutiny of that kind, however penetrating, will fit us to answer the question, " What think ye of Christ? Whose son is he? " The whole evidence must be grouped together. We must take into account the witness of the life, of the person, of the person revealed in the life. We must bring together the things said, and done, and taught, and endured. Little by little the testimony of each part, viewed in relation with the rest, will contribute to the ultimate decision on the whole. For that we must be content to wait. The ultimate decision must be made by each for himself. Not the baptism, or the temptation, or the teaching, or the ministry, or the incidental episodes, or even the crucifixion or the resurrection, can provide logical ground for belief or scepticism apart from the rest. Out of them all, each helping and contributing its share, will grow our view of the personality of Jesus Christ, will be shaped our individual answer to claims which challenge every living soul.

Therefore it is well worth while to review the evidence again; to place ourselves, as it were, in the company of the historic Jesus; to watch, to listen, and to learn. This, if we have reached a clear decision already, may confirm it. This, if we are yet at a loss for one, may bring it. Anyhow, it is a task worth while. It will be with the facts that we concern ourselves. Let the opinions about the facts form themselves; let them be based upon the evidence.

V

Thus (returning to the baptism) we will not delay to speculate over the relations of the divine and human in Jesus. Nor need we pause to consider whether the narrative of the signs—the opening of the heavens, the dove, the voice—is, or was meant to be, literally accurate. Possibly Jesus related this experience of his, like the experience of the temptations, in figurative language, language that best would reveal the intrinsic truth to his disciples. What is certain is that the baptism brought a spiritual crisis into the life of Jesus; that he became aware, if not for the first time, at least with a new sureness, of a divine mission and of supernatural powers. He knew himself to be the Christ, the promised Saviour. His work, as he now saw it, was to establish the heavenly kingdom, and to convince men of the truth which he had come to proclaim. How was that work best to be accomplished? What use was he to make of the powers with which he knew himself to be endowed? Before he began his public mission, he must decide once for all upon its character and scope.

Not with the Baptist, not with any of the friends who had accompanied him from Galilee, could he face this tremendous problem. He must think it out alone. Insidious and plausible ideas beset him, ideas of methods by which, as it seemed, the accomplishment of his life-work might be made easier. But were they right? Were they in accord with the will of his Father in heaven? In solitude he must decide. He had to realize in all its bearings the astounding revelation he had received at the Jordan. He must know how to use, how to abstain from misusing, the unique force which stirred within him. Therefore he withdrew into the wilderness, far from men, alone " with the wild beasts," to quote a graphic detail of the narrative which he himself must have supplied.

There, after fierce agony of mind, the plans were made. There the battle against temptations was fought and won. In after-days he told his friends of that experience, and described in vivid imagery the powerful

c

suggestions of evil which presented themselves, suggestions which in turn he
resisted and drove away.

First came the idea that he would most
readily gain the favour of the multitude if
he used his power for material ends. Might
they not listen more readily to his spiritual
message when he had secured their bodily
comfort? He had spent some thirty years
in a town of Galilee. Few of its inhabitants
were in easy circumstances. His own
family was not indigent, yet belonged to
that class which has no margin, is never free
from anxiety, and is unable to meet any
unforeseen demand on its resources. He
understood keenly, as his subsequent teaching was to prove, the strain and worry of
such conditions. He knew how anxiety
about the morrow was apt to absorb the
mind, to make it deaf to spiritual appeal.
He saw, too, a large number of people whose
conditions were far worse, beggars whose
lives were spent in misery, squalor, and
destitution. In bitter contrast were the

few rich men who fared sumptuously every day.

Here, then, seemed a short cut to the end he had in view. He might employ those supernatural powers of which he felt conscious in ending poverty and hunger. He could command the stones to become bread. Certainly that would draw the eyes of all to him, and give him a vast popularity. Thus, without danger and with no difficulties to overcome, he would have gained the ear of the public for whatever spiritual teaching he wished afterwards to give.

Yet his inner self knew this most plausible idea to be wrong. It seemed to make his task easy. In reality, it would make it impossible. It would emphasize the very idea he had come to overthrow, that material things were of a chief importance. He was to teach that man does not live by bread alone. He was to give the world a new set of values, in which the life of the spirit was to transcend all else. That must be difficult enough, but it would become

impossible had he been recognized as one
whose most important work was to relieve
bodily hunger. When later, in special circumstances, he did multiply food for those
who had listened to him, the result was that
people sought him, not from high motives,
" but because ye did eat of the loaves, and
were filled." At least his whole campaign
should not be hindered by an initial mistake
of that kind. He fought the temptation.
He mastered it.

To it succeeded another, as dangerous and
as plausible as the first. He, in the eyes
of the world an unknown peasant, had
somehow to gain its attention. Whatever
the wisdom of his message, no result would
follow unless he could gain a hearing for it.
Moreover, it would run counter to accepted
ideas. It would provoke the hostility of
every religious authority, whether Pharisee
or Sadducee. How could he hope for a
hearing? One way seemed obvious. He
could rely on his supernatural powers. He
could do things so dramatic, so striking,

that all the world would talk and wonder;
things like a sudden appearance on a
pinnacle of the Temple, whence he would
float down to an awestruck and worshipping
assemblage in the courts below. He was
sure that he possessed such powers, and we
can understand how intense was the temptation to put them to sensational use. By
other means, how slow at best must be his
progress! But by these within how short
a time would the multitudes be hanging
upon his every word! Yet he knew the
falsity of such reasoning. It was not as a
worker of spectacular prodigies that he
would be known among men. He desired
to persuade, not to astonish; not to dazzle
eyes or excite minds, but to transform
hearts. Again, he fought that temptation
and mastered it.

A third presented itself. A large proportion of the Jews expected the Messiah
to proclaim himself their king, to set himself
at the head of armies, and to lead them to
battle and conquest against the Empire

which held them in thrall. To be recognized as the Messiah, must he not fulfil those expectations? He could stir patriotism to its depths. The whole nation would rally to his call. With his powers, there was no limit to what he might achieve. He might pass from triumph to triumph, until Cæsar himself had made way for him. All the kingdoms of the world seemed to lie before him, and there was a voice which said, " All these things will I give thee, if——" . . . But not thus, not by violence and warfare, was the Kingdom of God to be set up, not thus was the Father's will to be done. Once more, he fought that temptation and mastered it.

Spent with that terrific mental conflict, but victorious, he returned from the wilderness.

VI

In past times some harm was done by describing this episode as " the temptation." The phrase encouraged a false idea that Jesus, having won this threefold victory in the wilderness, was exempt from temptation through the rest of his life. His own words refute that error, as when he praises his disciples because " ye are they which have continued with me in my temptations." Indeed, there can have been no day when he did not feel the pressure of temptation in some degree. Yet it must be true also that there was no day when his resistance to other temptations was not made easier by the victories in the wilderness at the outset of his career. And there was no day when the decisions then reached did not influence his methods.

That fact has to be remembered throughout our study of the Gospel narratives. With tranquil detachment, he seems to view material things as of small account. Inevitably he seems to reject every opportunity of using his powers in a sensational fashion to compel the homage of his countrymen. Serenely he turns from an excited crowd which would acclaim him as king in order that he may lead them in revolt. Thus we are apt to suppose that such lures had no attraction for him. On the contrary, each had appealed to him intensely. At the cost of tremendous effort, and after real agony, he had renounced them. He had faced and conquered them so thoroughly in the wilderness that afterwards they could not discompose him seriously. But only because of this great moral decision, and not easily or because they did not attract him, did he abstain from using them.

Thus the baptism had given Jesus a full consciousness of his mission. The temptations in the wilderness had shown certain plausible ways of attempting to accomplish it which he must not employ. But what was the right method? How was his great task to be done?

For a time, perhaps while his thoughts were shaping themselves into decision, Jesus remained with the Baptist. He helped in proclaiming the message of repentance. Some of his friends from Galilee, who had

been among John's disciples, now attached
themselves to Jesus—at the suggestion, it
seems, of the Baptist himself. They took
a share in baptizing the crowds that came
to the Jordan. Jesus himself did not. He
wished to support and endorse the work of
John, not to be accounted his rival. But
he was unable to prevent it. His wonderful
charm attracted many who were dismayed
by the stern austerity of John. The
numbers that thronged him grew, while the
hearers of John diminished. " All men
come to him ! " complained John's loyal
disciples, jealous for his fame. The great-
hearted Baptist rejoiced in the fact, believed
Jesus to be the Messiah and himself but the
Messiah's herald. " He must increase, but
I must decrease," he said.

Yet even an appearance of rivalry, as
Jesus saw, must hamper the special work
of the Baptist. Moreover, friction between
the two groups of disciples became inevitable. Soon there was the beginning of a
dispute between them about fasting, because

Jesus did not follow the ascetic rule of John. Evidently the time had come for a separation. The time had come, too, when Jesus must prepare to begin his own work. So far, he had been assisting a prophet and preaching as a prophet. In a sense, he would continue that work to the end. He would carry far beyond any other that insistence on personal character, on inward purity, on direct communion with God, which had been characteristic of the older prophets and had been revived by the Baptist. Such messages would not of themselves, however, suffice to meet the needs of his day. There was a wide range of subjects on which he must speak which lay outside the prophetic scope. Only the recognized religious teachers were allowed to handle them. Only they were allowed to touch the subjects comprised under the Law.

Jesus was resolved to end the old contrast and antagonism between the Law and the prophets. He was resolved, as he had told

John, to fulfil *all* righteousness; to interpret the true meaning of righteousness as contained by the Law and the prophets alike. He was not come, as he declared subsequently, to destroy either the Law or the prophetic message; he was come to " fulfil " —to fill full of meaning—both alike. He would be in the most favourable position to accomplish this if he approached the public as a Teacher of the Law. New and startling indeed his interpretation of it must seem. But thus best would his work be done.

So the choice was made. As yet he would make no proclamation of his Messiahship. He would not come forward as one claiming kingship, or as a revolutionary, or as a social reformer. Let the leaven work quietly from within. Presently the day for disclosure would come. Meanwhile he must teach. He must adopt outwardly the career of a rabbi. This, in the eyes of the world, was to be his profession. He would be Jesus the Teacher.

CHAPTER II

THE TEACHER

I

THE Gospels were designed, not as complete biographies of Jesus, but as records of his ministry. Therefore they are silent concerning his life between infancy and the beginning of public work at the age of thirty. As in all the four Gospels there is but one exception to this rule, we may be sure that the exception has some very special significance. It must have been admitted because it seemed to throw light upon the ministry itself.

St. Luke, who seems to have had it from the Mother of Jesus, gives us this episode. It is the familiar story of the boy Jesus among the doctors of the Law. On their return journey from the Passover at Jerusalem, Mary and Joseph discovered that he was not, as they had supposed, in the caravan from Nazareth. So they returned to Jerusalem, and, after a long search, found him among the rabbis in the Temple, " both hearing them and asking them questions." When they remonstrated, the boy answered, " How is it that ye sought me? Wist ye not that I must be in my Father's house? " And then he went with them to Nazareth.

Why was this solitary anecdote of the boyhood incorporated by St. Luke in his Gospel? Surely because it revealed the interests and ambition of Jesus as a child, and therefore illuminated his subsequent career. When he was but twelve the boy showed what he would like to be when he was grown up. He loved the Temple at his first sight of it. And, child as he was, he loved it not for its outward splendour, but for its inward and spiritual significance; " my Father's house," he termed it.[1] He

[1] The accuracy of the R.V. rendering " in my Father's house " (replacing the " about my Father's

felt drawn to the rabbis. He joined himself to their catechetical class, and astounded both them and the casual listeners by " his understanding and his answers." There, utterly absorbed, he was found by Mary and Joseph. Obediently, yet we may guess with what reluctance, he rose at their call and journeyed with them back to Nazareth.

But he had decided, as children will, what should be his profession ! The work of a religious teacher—that was his choice. Perhaps in those childish games, which he described long afterwards, when others played at weddings or funerals, the child Jesus ever liked best to play at being a rabbi with his class about him. At the time, few things could have seemed less likely than the fulfilment of the boy's wish. The rabbis belonged to a higher social class; Jesus would have to carry on Joseph's trade as a carpenter. Yet Mary

business " of the A.V.) has been strikingly confirmed more recently by the evidence of the papyri. See the Moulton–Milligan *Vocabulary of the Greek New Testament*, p. 209.

knew what her neighbours did not, and, like many a loving mother, she treasured the memory of her son's early words. She kept them in her heart, and long afterwards, when the boyish wish had been gloriously fulfilled, confided them to St. Luke. That at least seems to explain naturally the inclusion of this incident in his Gospel. It was not only striking and beautiful in itself; there must have been numberless incidents in the youth and early manhood of Jesus which deserved those adjectives. But it revealed, as did no other, the significant fact that at the age of twelve he had already set his heart upon that calling which afterwards he followed.

Yet the opportunity for taking it up was long deferred. As a child doubtless Jesus attended the school attached to the synagogue at Nazareth. Then, until he was about thirty years of age, he had to follow the trade of a carpenter. We cannot tell if some improvement in the family fortunes, or conceivably the disposal of the business after Joseph's death, set him free to join the Baptist by the Jordan. But when the baptism had brought clear consciousness of his messianic mission, and the struggle in the wilderness had made impossible the use of rapid and sensational methods for its accomplishment, the questions of the means he should employ must have confronted him afresh. The result was to strengthen his early idea. Not yet could his divine claims be put forward. Not yet could he assert himself publicly as the Messiah. His hour was not yet come. First, he must teach, and the teaching would reveal what he was to those who listened rightly and set themselves to obey. Not through outward proclamation, but through inward conviction, would grow faith of the kind he desired. For the present, he would sow the seed, he would set the leaven to work. He would be a teacher.

To be a religious teacher in Palestine at this period meant to join a clearly-defined profession, with its own position, mode of life, and carefully-guarded privileges. The point is often forgotten. Jesus in the eyes of his contemporaries was not a private individual, roaming about the country and discoursing casually with people he met. He was as definitely a teacher as Matthew had been a publican and Simon a fisherman. He was recognized as a member of a learned profession. By the general public, especially in the earlier stages of his work, he was unhesitatingly identified as a " scribe," as one of those authorized " teachers of the Law " to whom, as a sign of respect, the title of " rabbi " was accorded. This idea would be strengthened when his listeners heard him begin to speak on topics which these authorized teachers alone were permitted to handle. Yet, as they listened further, how vastly new and strange proved his treatment of the themes! Thus we are able to appreciate the real force of a sentence in the Gospels which is commonly misunderstood. They who heard him were

D

" increasingly astonished "—such is the exact force of the tense used—" at his teaching. For he taught as one having a scribe's authority, yet not as their scribes."

II

If we ask why Jesus chose to give this form to his work why he made himself known as a rabbi, despite the sharp contrast between his own and the rabbinic doctrines, answers are not difficult to suggest. This very unlikeness between his own teaching and the conventional beliefs of other " teachers of the Law " may have been a reason for his choice. He had begun as a fellow-worker with a prophet. When he delivered his own message, he might be not only misrepresented by his enemies, but misunderstood by his friends as an opponent of the Law. What he said must be so new, startling, and unexpected that it might be construed as an attack upon the Law which formed the foundation of the

Jewish creed.   Yet it was not to the Law
but to legalism that he was opposed.   So
far from attacking the Law, he said, he
had come to give it new force and to fulfil
it.   Not one jot or tittle of it should pass
away.   He would show that its claims were
far more pervasive, and went far deeper
below the surface of life, than its conventional exponents imagined.   To overcome
the initial suspicion that he was hostile to
the Law, he could take no course more
effectual than to appear as a rabbi, as one
of the Law's accredited champions and
interpreters.

Again, unless he were recognized as a
rabbi, he would be debarred from handling
many subjects about which new teaching
was most needed.   Any person thought
competent, any layman as we should say,
might speak, even in the synagogue, about
religion in general, and questions of morals
or ethics.   These were considered of less
importance.   But the Law and the traditions were a province strictly confined to

the rabbis. Unless he had appeared as a rabbi, it would have been impossible for Jesus to teach publicly, as he desired to do, concerning such matters as marriage, prayer, fasting, and the observance of the sabbath, or to discuss the traditions—the things " said by them of old time." But as a recognized rabbi he would be expected to treat such themes. As a matter of course, too, he would be invited to address the congregation by the rulers of each synagogue he visited. Thus the profession he chose gave Jesus freedom of speech, and made it easier for him to ensure a hearing, during the earlier days of his ministry.

It had other advantages as well. He desired to journey about the country accompanied by disciples. They were to be his friends, whose love would be his solace. They were to be also the earliest members of that society he designed to found, which should transmit and spread his message when his own ministry on earth was over. It was the common practice of rabbis to surround themselves with groups of disciples, and to travel in their company. Thus, as a rabbi, Jesus was able to fulfil his purpose, and stirred no suspicion by doing so. But this would have been very difficult had he not been accounted a religious teacher. Almost inevitably he and the group of men surrounding him would have been suspect. Roman officials would have supposed them to be conspirators, engaged in propagating sedition.

Finally, to work as a rabbi solved for Jesus the problem of subsistence. It was a common custom for prominent rabbis to be maintained by devout women of wealth. Of this custom he availed himself, and St. Luke's Gospel records the names of some who " ministered of their substance," and thus provided for the simple needs of Jesus and his disciples. It was a custom open to abuse, and Jesus denounced those rabbis who " devoured widows' houses." But those whose help he accepted were wealthy, and by this means he was able to concentrate wholly upon his mission, and was set free from the necessity of manual labour.

Thus after baptism and temptation Jesus determined to work as a rabbi, and to teach until the time came for him to announce himself publicly as the Messiah. The Gospel narratives become far more luminous when we remember this fact. Small details become significant. He sits down to speak to his disciple or the multitude; a rabbi stood to pray or read; when he sat down, it was a sign that he was about to give instruction. Jesus, the well-known rabbi, handled freely themes with which none but a rabbi was allowed to deal. Like other rabbis, he clothed much of his instruction in parables—though how different were his from the others! When some pupil answered a question particularly well, a rabbi's custom was to show his approval by kissing the speaker. So Jesus did to a rich young man whose words pleased him, and thus we understand what is meant by the phrase of our English version which states that " Jesus, looking upon him, loved him." Again, our English version, by using the ambiguous word " Master," obscures the fact that it was as " Rabbi "—" which is to say, Teacher "— that Jesus was habitually addressed, by friends and enemies alike.

We may realize easily the amazement which Jesus stirred among the people of his time. Here, to all appearance, was a scribe. He lived and worked as a scribe. Yet his teaching was utterly at variance with the scribes' doctrine, and of the scribes themselves he spoke with withering denunciation. No wonder that the people were at once attracted and bewildered. No wonder that the scribes soon plotted to bring about his downfall.

III

The writers of the Gospels purposely limited themselves, as we have seen, to describing the ministry of Jesus, instead of attempting a full account of his life. Therefore its exact chronology at many points is obscure, and there have been elaborate controversies about it, as unprofitable as they are laborious. It seems clear, however, that there were three years between the baptism and the crucifixion. But then we are confronted by the strange fact that, after the temptation in the wilderness, all the events described by the synoptic Gospels—*i.e.*, St. Mark, St. Matthew, and St. Luke—belong to the last two of these three years. Of the first year they say nothing. Only from the Fourth Gospel we gather that, with the exception of a visit lasting " not many days " to Galilee, this year was spent in Jerusalem and its neighbourhood. And all that this Gospel attributes to the first year comes within its first four months. Three of the Gospels are silent about the whole year; the Fourth is silent about eight months of it.

What is the cause of this gap? How

are we to account for this "year of obscurity," as it is often termed? Various explanations have been put forward. One is that the Evangelists were silent simply because they had no information about the events of the year. This, however, if the year were one of active ministry, seems most improbable. Another theory is that before beginning his work in Galilee Jesus felt bound to deliver his message first in Jerusalem itself, and the Fourth Gospel indicates that he spent the time in Jerusalem and Judæa. But there, it is argued, he had no success. He failed to make any impression upon the people of Jerusalem, and accordingly, after many months of unsuccessful effort, migrated to the north country of Galilee. The Evangelists, if we accept this theory, "passed by his activity at the headquarters of the nation as a work with merely negative results "[1] and concentrated upon describing the later

[1] The phrase is taken from Dr. Stalker's *Life of Jesus Christ.*

and more successful Galilæan ministry.
Yet it seems unlikely that the failure in
Jerusalem would have been so complete.
It is unlikely that many months of work
would have brought about no incident
worthy of record. And it is most unlikely
that, even were the failure quite unre-
deemed, the Evangelists would not, with
their habitual candour, have written a
sentence or two admitting this fact, and
epitomizing the many months it covered.

The point which we have reached in the
story of Jesus seems to suggest another
explanation. It seems simpler to believe
that the writers whose chosen task was to
describe his ministry began their account
with his arrival in Galilee because it was
then that his ministry began. But how,
then, were the previous eight months
occupied? Almost inevitably, we may
think, in preparing for the work. Jesus
was exchanging the occupation of an artisan
for a learned profession. He was about to
come before the world as a rabbi. We

recall again that early episode of his boyhood, when he joined himself to the rabbis' class in the Temple. It had stirred his childish interest. It would have a stronger attraction now. Would he not now renew that experience, studying closely both the methods, many of which he was himself to employ, and the doctrine, with so much of which he could not agree? He would desire to acquaint himself thoroughly with the official religious teaching of his time, in order that he might confirm what was right in it, and rectify what was wrong. He would require to be thoroughly versed both in the Law itself, and in the traditions which were held to interpret it.

For this purpose, he would need to learn the language in which the Scriptures were written. The spoken language of the time was Aramaic. A large proportion of the Jews were bi-lingual, and spoke Greek also. It seems almost certain that Jesus himself could speak Greek, though Aramaic was his habitual tongue. But the Scriptures were written in Hebrew. The working-class Jews did not know Hebrew. Therefore when Scripture was read aloud in the synagogue services, an interpreter stood beside the reader, translating what the other read in Hebrew into the Aramaic which the people understood.

It seems most unlikely that Jesus would have had any opportunity of learning Hebrew during his childhood, when he attended what we should now term an " elementary " school, or during the years that he worked as a carpenter. Yet early in his Galilæan ministry he officiated at a synagogue service in Nazareth and read from the synagogue roll—written, of course, in Hebrew—a portion of Isaiah. By this time, therefore, certainly he knew Hebrew. It seems reasonable to suppose that he acquired this, with much other learning, during the previous months at Jerusalem.

No doubt, such an attempt to explain " the year of obscurity " must remain, like any other, incapable of proof. Yet the claim may be ventured for it that it does seem to fit the facts. Let us imagine the active ministry to have begun immediately after Jesus had left the Baptist. Perplexing questions would at once suggest themselves. Where and when had he obtained his close acquaintance with rabbinical customs and doctrines? How could he who had lived and worked to the age of thirty as an artisan suddenly appear, and be accepted without question as, a member of a learned profession? It would be necessary to suppose that some wholly miraculous means of acquiring knowledge were bestowed upon him—a theory which even we who admit most fully his divine claims would be loth to accept. Not merely would it conflict with that gradual "increase in wisdom" which St. Luke was careful to record, but it would mar the perfect humanity we reverence. His matchless skill and knowledge as a teacher would compel less, not more, admiration from us were they attained without effort. But the

" year of obscurity " provides a simple way of escape from such difficulties. It seems natural to conclude that through these months, spent mainly in Jerusalem, Jesus was training himself for the form of ministry he had decided to adopt. He was thinking things out, and observing, and studying themes and methods. He was learning in order that he might teach. He never grudged time spent in preparing himself for the great turning-points in his life. At length this task was done. He had decided upon the methods he would use. The technical knowledge required was his. He had examined intimately the official religion of his day, and discerned the reasons of its failure. He was equipped to come forward, no longer as a carpenter, but as a rabbi. The ministry, and with it the Gospels' record of the ministry, began.

IV

The Gospels make quite clear what was the immediate cause of the beginning. News came that Herod, the ruler of Galilee, had arrested and imprisoned the Baptist. At once Jesus hastened to Galilee and preached there. After the first thirteen verses of his Gospel, which summarize the story of the Baptist's mission and the baptism and temptation of Jesus, St. Mark opens his main narrative in this characteristic fashion :

Now after that John was delivered up, Jesus came into Galilee, preaching the gospel of God, and saying, The time is fulfilled and the kingdom of God is at hand : repent ye, and believe in the gospel.

The austere restraint of that matter-of-fact sentence conceals the heroism of the action it describes. Herod Antipas suspected the announcement of a new " kingdom " at hand to be the language of a revolutionary. Therefore he threw John into prison. At once Jesus hastened into Herod's territory to repeat what the Baptist had said. It was a direct challenge to Herod. It was a contemptuous proof that John's imprisonment would not check the spreading of John's message. And it was the first of the many acts of magnificent courage recorded of Jesus in the Gospels.

Too often readers fail to discern them, being misled by the tranquil language. " After that John was delivered up, Jesus came into Galilee "—it is only when we pause to consider what the words involve that we realize the intrepidity set before us. The charm, the tenderness, the sympathy of Jesus—these are readily seen by every reader of the Gospels. But their unemotional language leaves us to perceive for ourselves that indomitable courage without which any idea of his character must be pitifully false. Artists also, perhaps, by their conventional portraits, have accen-

tuated so much the wistful gentleness of
Jesus that they have obscured his majestic
strength.

Indeed the peril he faced by entering
Herod's territory was very real, and increased throughout his stay there. Here
again the tranquil language of the Gospels
is apt to mislead us. As Dr. Headlam [1]
has shown, many of the journeys with
disciples were no leisurely preaching tours,
but forced movements to escape Herod's
emissaries. Else the work of Jesus, like
that of John, would have been brought to
a premature end. The time for the announcement of his Messiahship must come
first.

So Jesus travelled from Jerusalem to
Galilee, to reiterate John's message and to
begin his own work as a rabbi. He made
his home at Capernaum. Why there, rather
than at Nazareth? Partly because the
people of Nazareth were jealous of him, and

[1] In his Belden Noble lectures, *Jesus Christ in
History and Faith*. (1925.)

E

the home atmosphere there was difficult, with brethren who mocked his words. Partly because his first disciples and closest friends, who had been with him in the south by the Jordan, had their homes at Capernaum. But also because Capernaum stood on the shore of the Sea of Galilee. The opposite coast was outside the control of Herod Antipas and under the rule of Philip, a far more amiable character. From Capernaum, therefore, Jesus could escape quickly in case of threatened arrest. With a view to such an emergency the disciples kept one of their boats in readiness. Not only as a matter of convenience did Jesus use it when he preached to the multitudes on the beach. Should news come that Herod's officials were approaching, at once the disciples compel their master to embark, and take him swiftly out of Herod's jurisdiction.

Having confirmed the Baptist's message, and having endorsed in this way the teaching of the last and greatest prophet, Jesus

entered upon his own work of reinterpreting
the Law. At first he was invited by the
rulers of the synagogues, like other visiting
rabbis, to take part in the services and to
address the congregations. " He spake in
their synagogues, being glorified of all."
Afterwards there came a change of method.
His vast influence upon the people stirred
the jealousy of the official religious teachers,
and they would not allow him to be heard
in the synagogues. Even if they had, the
multitudes which habitually thronged to
hear him were far larger than any building
could contain. Of necessity, therefore, Jesus
gave much of his later teaching out-of-doors.
But we get a quite false idea of the early
ministry if we suppose that Jesus appeared
to his listeners as a kind of unauthorized
lay preacher, apart from, or even hostile to,
the religious organizations of his age. Later
on, it is true, official jealousy forced him
into something like that position. At the
outset, however, no one who came to hear
him doubted that he was coming to hear

the teaching of a rabbi—most unexpected
and most startling as the teaching of this
rabbi proved to be.

Soon after he had begun his work, he
visited Nazareth,[1] and here he first met
with hostility. The facts we have been
considering explain it. Some of his fellow-
townsmen in the synagogue of Nazareth
were profoundly impressed by the charm
both of his message and his manner. But,
among others, the chief feeling was one of
resentment at his reappearance among them,
not as the artisan they had known, but as
a rabbi. If some distinguished teacher of
the Law visited Nazareth, by all means let
him occupy the seat of authority in their
synagogue. It was a very different matter,
they argued, when one of their own number,
of the same social rank and education as
themselves, presumed to come back as a
member of a learned profession and claimed

[1] " It was not a private visit to his family; he came
as a rabbi, surrounded by his scholars."—Dr. Swete,
Commentary on St. Mark, vi. 1.

to instruct them. Where had he got his knowledge? What were these stories of mighty works attributed to him? " Why, we know all about him," they said. " ' Is not this the carpenter, the son of Mary, and brother of James and Joses and Judas and Simon? And are not his sisters here with us? ' And they were offended in him."

Jesus, the Evangelist adds, " marvelled because of their unbelief." He quoted the proverb that only in his own country, and among those who know him well, is the teacher unhonoured. They failed to realize, these comrades of his younger years, the vast change that had befallen him. He had lived among them as Jesus the carpenter. That time was past. The day would come when he must publicly enter the capital as Jesus the Christ. Meanwhile, he would be known as Jesus the rabbi. Some, even as he taught, would have their eyes opened, would discern for themselves the final and overwhelming truth about

him.   Others at least would be made more
ready for its disclosure.   He must teach
the laws of the Kingdom and the conditions
of entry to it before the Kingdom itself
could be proclaimed.

CHAPTER III

THE TEACHING BY WORD

I

THE work of Jesus in Galilee seems to have extended over two years. It is possible to mark certain definite stages in it, and to see how its conditions altered as time went on. But it is not possible to place all the events described by the Gospels in their strict sequence of time. The writers of the Gospels made no attempt to supply a day-by-day diary. The happenings of a month or more are sometimes compressed into a few sentences, or even omitted entirely. We can say that probably chronological order is followed more closely by St. Mark than by the other Evangelists. All of them, however, were far more anxious to make clear the teaching of Jesus than to set forth the precise moment at which each part of that teaching was given. In other words, their habit was to group sayings upon one subject, or incidents illuminating some special point in his doctrine, even though the sayings were spoken and the incidents occurred at considerable intervals. Again, what is brought before us apparently as a connected discourse may consist sometimes of various utterances originally spoken at various times and in various places.

This has long since been recognized by scholars, and, with it, the fact that any attempt to reconstruct exactly the story of these years must needs be full of what are, at best, probable surmises. Another point —and of this scholars seem more apt to be forgetful—is that Jesus is most unlikely to have given the most important parts of his teaching on one occasion only. One of the most common type of supposed New Testament problems is caused when St. Matthew (let us say) records some special piece of teaching as given in one setting, while St. Luke attributes it to another place and occasion. All the learned arguments that follow are based on the assumption that Jesus could not have said the same things twice, in slightly varied forms. Yet how strange his action if he did not ! We know that the rabbis repeated over and over, and made their disciples learn by heart, the principles to which they attached special importance. We may feel confident that Jesus, teaching as a rabbi, would follow this method. He was travelling from place to place. He was continually instructing new audiences. Are we to imagine that he would never use again some parable which had served particularly well to enforce his point, or that many of those marvellously compact sentences summarizing main points in his doctrine—such as the " Beatitudes," for example—were not spoken by him time and time again ?

After all, however, it is the things said by Jesus that matter. Whether any particular saying was said on this occasion, or on that—or, as well may be, on both—is of far less importance. In these pages, at least, we need not concern ourselves with such discussions. We will not try to arrange in strict chronological sequence the various episodes related by the various Evangelists. Our aim here will be quite different. It will be to place ourselves, so far as we can, among those who first listened to Jesus, to share their points of view, to understand the effect of his words upon them. Putting aside, as far as possible, all prepossessions, we will watch, and listen, and learn, studying the teacher in relation with his age and his surroundings.

II

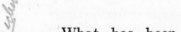

What has been written already may serve to remove one quite false idea which is still very common. People imagine Jesus appearing to his contemporaries as one of the very poor, as a carpenter who left his work and travelled about Palestine in almost abject poverty as a kind of self-constituted lay evangelist. That may be an attractive picture. But emphatically it is not the picture given by the Gospels when these are rightly understood. It is true that Jesus had been a carpenter. Yet he was a recognized member of a learned profession when his ministry began at Capernaum. " Rabbi, we know that thou art a teacher sent from God " was the way in which Nicodemus addressed him at a first meeting. That was not the fashion in which one of the chief Pharisees, a member of the Jewish Council, would speak to a carpenter! In the last week of his life, at Jerusalem, his credentials as an authorized rabbi were challenged: "By what kind of authority doest thou these things, and who gave thee that authority?" —but until that time they seem to have been admitted without serious demur even by his opponents. They attacked bitterly his teaching, but not his authority as a teacher. Indeed, their resentment was the greater because it was, as they supposed, from a rabbi himself that there came the scathing exposure of rabbinism.

Again, Jesus was not one of the very poor. His sympathy with the poor was wonderful, yet he never identifies himself with them. " Blessed are ye "—not " we " —" poor," is his word, and " the poor ye have always with you, but me ye have not always." His first disciples, a group of fishermen from the Sea of Galilee, were themselves employers of hired servants and moderately well-to-do. During their travels with Jesus they were supported, as we have noted, by gifts from wealthy adherents, as were other rabbis and their companions. Often they were welcome guests in rich men's houses. Jesus had indeed his ups and downs of worldly fortune, and, as the opposition of the religious authorities and of Herod increased, many became afraid to show him hospitality. Thus there came at least one moment when he had nowhere

to lay his head. Yet to use that pathetic
phrase as though it described the normal
condition of the life of Jesus is simply to
ignore the evidence of the Gospels.

Jesus was seldom houseless. But almost
throughout his years of ministry he was
homeless. This, unlike poverty, must have
been one of the severest trials in his life.
No longer had he any place in the household
at Nazareth. His brethren derided him.
Even his mother feared for his reason.
He secured a lodging in the house of one of
his fishermen-friends at Capernaum. Towards the very end he did find another
home, full of welcome and tenderness and
peace, at Bethany. How often, though,
through the intervening years of work,
Jesus must have craved a home! How
seldom he was allowed quiet and privacy!
He had great need of both, not only for
rest, but for prayer, and thought, and the
planning of his work, and the preparation
of his teaching. " But thou, when thou
prayest," he counselled, " enter into thine

inner chamber, and having shut thy door "
. . . Practicable enough for others, not for
himself, who had no solitude in an inner
chamber at his command! All he could
contrive was to escape sometimes to the
lonely hills behind Capernaum for thought
and prayer. Even that had to be done
under the befriending darkness of night;
else before long his disciples, perhaps with
a crowd at their heels, would come hurrying
to the place where he was.

The immense and immediate success, as
it seemed, of his work in Galilee was to
prove a vast hindrance to its accomplishment as Jesus desired, and an enormous
strain upon the teacher.

III

For the effect produced from the first by
the teaching of Jesus was vast. He began,
as we have seen, in the synagogue of
Capernaum. Very soon his fame had gone
far beyond the limits of that town. Crowds

flocked into it from the neighbouring places, simply that they might see and hear this wonderful rabbi. What, we may wonder, was the " report of him " which, in St. Mark's phrase, " went out straightway everywhere into all the region of Galilee round about "? What gave Jesus this attractive power?

It was not any declaration of his Messiahship. Had he proclaimed himself the expected Christ, that would have accounted fully for any degree of popular excitement. But, in point of fact, fully conscious of his Messiahship though he was, he made as yet no public announcement of it. The hour was not yet come. Much teaching must be given first. Once only, in the synagogue of Nazareth, he ventured on a tentative disclosure, by reading certain messianic prophecies of Isaiah and applying them to himself. Promptly he was cast out of the synagogue and an attempt was made upon his life; the result, no doubt, of local jealousy. But it served to emphasize the risks of a premature disclosure. Had he plainly revealed himself in Capernaum as the Messiah, immediately he would have brought popular feeling to a fever-heat. Some who heard would immediately have tried to assassinate him as a dangerous blasphemer. But a far greater number would have hailed him with frantic enthusiasm, would have tried—as on a later day a concourse did try—to make him their king, would have flocked to him as the leader of an immediate national revolt against Rome.

Therefore Jesus kept his secret. He did not claim to be the Messiah in his teaching. Even his close companions did not yet suspect it. When, before long, some were startled into a dawning conviction that this must be none other than the Christ, he insisted that they should not spread abroad their belief. Evidently, then, it was not by any announcement of himself as the Messiah that he attracted the multitudes in Galilee.

Many were drawn by his repute as a healer. The use of his powers in this way was indeed an essential part of his scheme of teaching; his teaching healed, and his healing taught. Its full significance is a point which we shall have to consider presently. But at this stage we should observe that the works of healing were not in the early days of the ministry the chief factor in gathering the crowds that surrounded Jesus. Primarily, these people came, not to see the things he did, but to hear the words he said. They had been told of him as a wonderful rabbi. He attracted them as a teacher who sometimes healed, not as a healer who sometimes taught. When he was in Capernaum, they filled the synagogue, they thronged him for hours at a time on the beach. If they heard that he had retreated to the hills, they pursued him there indefatigably, they invaded a private house where he was known to be, " so that there was no longer room for them, no, not even about the

F

door." When he had undergone the strain of speaking to a concourse in the open air for hour after hour and was utterly worn out, they were still craving for more. The disciples, seeing his fatigue, hurried him into their boat and set off for the other side, and so profound was his sleep of exhaustion that not even the tumult of a hurricane could wake him. Yet some of his audience also embarked in boats, in the desperate hope that he would teach again on the opposite shore.

When he travelled, the inhabitants of each town or village he entered clustered eagerly about him. Simply that they might listen to this teacher, pilgrims came to Galilee from north and south. They came from the distant ports of Tyre and Sidon, cities with heathen populations. They came from the country about Jordan, from Judæa and from Jerusalem itself. The Evangelists record these facts with the utmost simplicity. But when we illuminate their

succinct narrative by consulting a map,
by noting the distances travelled and by
remembering the difficulties of travel, we
begin to realize what passionate enthusiasm
there was to hear Jesus during the early
days of his ministry. When, again, we
look for the causes producing this effect,
when we enquire what it was that attracted
and fascinated those who listened to him,
the Gospels give us an explicit answer. It
was the novelty of his message. New
rabbis going a round of the provincial
synagogues were common enough. But
none of them spoke as this man. Here was
not merely a new teacher, but a new teaching. It is easy for us, after nineteen
Christian centuries, to forget how amazingly
novel the fundamental doctrines of Jesus—
doctrines we have come to regard as ethical
truisms—appeared to the folk who first
heard them. Yet their feelings are vividly
depicted by the Evangelists. Those who
listened were " increasingly astonished."

They were " all amazed," reports St. Mark,
and " they questioned among themselves,
saying, ' What is this? A new teaching! ' "

IV

In what way was it new? Here, once
more, we have need to distinguish. It was
a novelty, not of theme, but of treatment.
When a stranger drew near to the seated
teacher, and had worked his way through
the crowd until at last he came within
earshot, probably enough there would be
no surprise in the first impressions he
received. This rabbi was speaking of the
things about which rabbis were expected
to speak. In fact, they were the authorized
exponents of such themes. " Prayer,"
" fasting," " alms," " the sabbath," " the
great commandments of the Law "—as the
listener caught such words, he would com-
pose himself to receive instruction of the
normal rabbinical kind. Or the first words
that reached him might be " the kingdom

of God," when he would know that the theme of the moment was one which figured largely in the religious discussions of the time. But after a few sentences the casual listener's tranquil expectation would be changed to startled wonder. " What is this? a new teaching ! " The old themes were being handled in a way amazingly new.

Here indeed we touch what was the chief characteristic of Jesus as a teacher. In the ultimate sense, he was far less an innovator than an interpreter and revealer. He neither destroyed any essential part of the accepted creed of his age nor did he add any new articles to it. " Not to destroy, but to fulfil " was the keynote of his method. What he did was to take the current creed and ideals and religious institutions of the Jews and reveal in them a vital power and significance that no one else had suspected. Whether the point was the fundamental belief in God, or such a detail of life as the right use of

the sabbath, Jesus disclosed to his astonished hearers the real worth and dynamic
power of the creed already in their possession. It was, as we have seen, an age of
spiritual hunger. It was a time when the
masses craved eagerly some form of religion
which should make God real, and duty an
inspiration, and life an opportunity of
happy service, and the divine kingdom
more than a distant dream. And then
came Jesus, not to give them a new religion,
but to show that what they had already
could satisfy all their needs when once its
true contents were discerned. The excitement of listening to this teacher was the
excitement of discovering that the wealth
you had craved for years was already yours,
only you had never perceived it until your
eyes were opened.

There came a day when Jesus set forth
this truth by an acted parable. A pathetic
and weary multitude lacked food. How
should they be fed in the wilderness?
Jesus answered the question with another:

" How many loaves have ye ? " and bade
his disciples use what already was with
them. He blessed it and gave to his
disciples, the disciples gave to the multitude, and it sufficed to feed all. Not
otherwise did he use the religion of his day
to satisfy spiritual hunger.

He took the Law. All who listened
thought they knew what the Law meant.
It stood for an arid, impersonal code, made
yet more difficult and complicated by the
mass of rabbinic traditions. It stood for a
disheartening series of prohibitions. It
stood for a system which identified righteousness with external observances and absten-
tions. It stood for a kind of religion which
satisfied the Pharisees and proved an in-
tolerable burden to ordinary folk. But
how different the Law seemed when Jesus
had expounded it ! So far from over-
throwing it, he gave it a far greater importance than before. He revealed it as no
mere code, but as the voice of the living
God. From the mere letter its province

was extended to the realms of the spirit.
It touched the heart, the will, and the
conscience. It dominated motives and desires, not outward actions only. Fasting
and almsgiving, in place of being mere
ritual observances, became deeds of filial
service. Prayer was no longer an imposed
ceremony; it became the language of a
child speaking to his Father. Those who
listened to the teaching of Jesus felt that
never before had they understood the real
worth and power and constraining appeal
of the Law. Never had they seen it thus,
fraught with divine wisdom, and radiant
with love.

As thus he filled the Law with new meaning, so also he fulfilled the message of
the prophets. They, and the apocalyptic
writers after them, had looked forward to
the kingdom of God. The near approach
of that kingdom had been the ground of
the Baptist's call to repentance. The kingdom of God was a phrase with which every
Jew was familiar. But the interpretations

of it varied. Many linked it with a political revolt against Rome. Others thought of it as it was pictured in the apocalyptic visions, as coming with an end of the existing age, heralded by angels and trumpets and mystic signs, and with the revelation of God enthroned for judgment. Jesus also used and adapted to his purpose the apocalyptic writings, and this looking forward to a final manifestation and judgment is specially prominent in the Matthæan account of his teaching. But, as he interpreted the phrase, " the kingdom of God " meant also something far more immediate. It meant the reign of God in human souls and the union of those who combined to do his bidding. To the people who came to him, " the kingdom of God " had represented a political programme, or a mystical vision, or a blend of the two. But to the people who had heard him it was spiritual, not political, in its character ; it was of the present, and not of the future only, in its setting. The idea was so great and pervasive that Jesus himself could not easily set forth its full significance. He used one illustration after another in order to reveal some of its many aspects. No single parable could express more than a part of its rich comprehensiveness. Yet at least his hearers understood that to lead, individually and socially, the kind of life he described and to gain the character he depicted, was to find a place, here and now, in the kingdom of God. Again Jesus proved himself the revealer. Again he had taken a term with which they were familiar, and astonished them by showing what power and inspiration it contained.

V

Thus we can readily understand the vast impression Jesus made in Galilee, and the attractiveness of his teaching. It revealed God, and life, and religion as they had never been seen before. Legalism had proved a hopeless creed, but Jesus justified love of the Law when he disclosed in it the

law of love. He changed the prophetic
Kingdom of God from a vague aspiration
to a present reality. God had been conceived as an inexorable judge, or even as an
unimaginable pedant—for some of the rabbis
gravely affirmed that God spent three hours
daily in studying the Law! Now He was
made known as a Father who cared for
each individual soul, who took thought for
even the lowliest of created things.

We cannot suppose, of course, that the
full richness and implications of such teaching were evident at once. The first feeling
it stirred was bewilderment. Its hearers
were " exceedingly amazed," to quote the
frank record of the evangelists. How,
indeed, should they not be? This new
revelation was utterly unlike the authorized
teaching they had received from other
rabbis since their earliest days. We, on
the other hand, inured to Christian thought
by centuries of tradition, find it hard to
recapture that sense of novelty, do not
easily realize the shock which almost every

sentence of Christian doctrine held for its
audience by the Sea of Galilee or in the
synagogue of Capernaum. Yet eager multitudes were convinced by this " new teaching " of the strange rabbi. And none were
unmoved.

For there is a further point which, in
even the briefest summary, must not be
overlooked. To reveal God and His Kingdom to man was not all that the teaching
of Jesus did. It did something more; it
revealed man to himself. No doubt mere
curiosity first drew from their homes the
crowds that streamed from all parts to hear
this rabbi, of whose doctrine such strange
rumours had reached them. But, as they
listened, perhaps almost every man and
woman of them experienced two sensations
in turn. The first was an uncomfortable
dissatisfaction. Conscience awoke. The
accustomed standards were shown to be
false. These searching enquiries into hidden
motive, this new force given to the old
commandments, stirred a deep sense of

failure. Yet hard upon this sense of past failure followed a marvellous hope of future achievement. The quiet, persuasive voice to which they listened had a strange power. Beyond question, this rabbi knew what was in man. His appeal was based on human knowledge and experience: " What man of you " was a recurrent phrase in it. But he did not merely make them conscious of their shortcomings, or picture a new and noble kind of life, built upon a direct relationship with God. Not merely did he do this, but he insisted that his ideal was eminently practicable. He discerned in them powers and possibilities with which they had never dared to credit themselves. He made them feel strong. As they listened, these ordinary men and women were compelled to believe in themselves, because this teacher, with his unquestionable knowledge of human nature, so evidently believed in them.

Thus this ministry of teaching began and went on. The strain it imposed on the teacher must have been enormous. Every day was full, and it is evident that the public discourses were supplemented both by more detailed expositions given to the increasing body of disciples and by private interviews, of which a few only are recorded. St. Mark describes with some completeness a sabbath day in Capernaum, on the eve of a tour to other places. It began with long teaching at the synagogue service. Then a man "with an unclean spirit" was cured. After leaving the synagogue, Jesus and his disciples went to Simon's house. He was told that Simon's mother-in-law had fallen ill; at his touch "the fever left her, and she ministered unto them." A few hours later, as the shadows lengthened, a vast number of ailing folk were brought to the house, "and all the city was gathered together at the door." Again he healed and taught. It must have been late before he was able to get any rest. Yet in the morning, "a great while before day," he rose up, "and went out and departed into a desert place, and there prayed. And Simon and they that were with him followed after him. And they found him, and say unto him : All are seeking thee." So, with cheerful readiness, he began the next day's work, which marked the beginning of a short tour away from Capernaum. " Let us go elsewhere into the next towns," he said, " that I may preach there also, for to this end came I forth." And so " he went into their synagogues throughout all Galilee."

Yet, despite their toil, these were happy days. Jesus was accompanied, not merely by his few intimate friends, but by an increasing number of disciples, content to leave for a time all their normal occupations in order to be with him and hear his words. In their lives he could see his influence at work. Beyond them, again, were the great multitudes. As yet many of them may have understood but little, yet all were eager to learn. The hostility of the official religious leaders had not yet declared itself, and the time for challenging the world by a proclamation of Messiahship was not yet come. Enough for the present that the rabbi taught and the people listened. Of much concerning him they were ignorant, of much were doubtful. But that never man spake as this man they were increasingly sure.

CHAPTER IV

THE TEACHING BY DEED

I

IT is evident that Jesus was not satisfied by the mere outward success of his work in Galilee. Crowds came to hear him, and hung eagerly upon his words, and felt their power. But how far was their true meaning understood? How far was their effect transient? How far would the hearers not only listen with approval and interest, but adopt the teaching as their rule of life? Jesus knew the fickleness of human nature; he knew how many " when they have heard the word, straightway receive it with joy, but have no root in themselves." And the danger of achieving merely superficial results was increased when he began to travel from place to place. So long as he was continually in one synagogue, teaching the same people day after day, and living in the same town with them, he could explain special points that had perplexed them, he could insist in detail upon the practical consequences which acceptance of his doctrine must involve, and he could keep in personal touch with many at least of his hearers.

Conditions were changed when he left Capernaum and toured through the towns and villages. In each place his stay was brief. In each place he faced a new audience. The risk in these conditions was inevitably greater that the people who flocked to hear him would be charmed by a unique personality, would listen with wonder, interest, and enthusiasm to his message, but would not be much influenced by it in any practical way when he had departed elsewhere. Yet his aim was to touch not their emotions or their intellect so much as their will. Abstract doctrine was what they expected from a rabbi. A large proportion of rabbinical instruction was devoted to examining general principles in relation with hypothetical cases of conduct. What commandments should be ranked among the "greater," and what among the "less"? Supposing a pious Jew found himself in this or the other imagined position, which of two plausible courses would the Law, interpreted by tradition, direct him to take? Supposing, again, that the Law seemed to enjoin a moral duty—such as the support of aged parents —which proved inconvenient, by what device of casuistry—such as that of pleading "Corban"—could the duty be evaded? Of such themes the rabbis discoursed almost interminably. They won applause by their dialectical ingenuity in dealing with abstract cases, by their hair-splitting distinctions and sophistries.

Jesus had to convince a large audience in a short time that, though he appeared to them as a rabbi, his purpose was different. He was unconcerned with abstract doctrines. He set forward new interpretations both of the Law and of the prophetic message, but only that his hearers might apply these interpretations in practical conduct. He disclosed the true force of the Law in order that it should be made a rule of life. He revealed the true idea of the Kingdom in order that people should make themselves fit for places within it. And therefore to emphasize his doctrine, to make it yet more vivid, and to show it in action, as he travelled through Galilee he supplemented his teaching by word with teaching by deed.

II

For example, we may consider his instruction about the sabbath. This was a subject on which he spoke often during the first year of his ministry. Indeed, it was one concerning which he must have had to answer frequent questions. If many of the rabbinic doctrines were remote from the

ordinary life of the ordinary Jew, here was
one which must needs affect him in a very
practical way. Once a week the sabbath
came round, and once a week he must either
obey or evade the prescribed rules for
its observance. They were extraordinarily
complicated. On no subject had more
rabbinic ingenuity been expended. On no
subject was there a wider gulf between the
simple directions of the original Law, and
the elaborate traditions which ultimately
superseded it. The literature on the subject was voluminous. Two or three of the
rabbinic interpretations will show the type
of rules they made and distinctions they
drew. When the disciples walking through
a cornfield on the sabbath plucked ears of
wheat, such action was classified as " work,"
and therefore was held to involve grave
sin. A woman might not look in a mirror
on the sabbath. If she did, she might
notice a grey hair and be tempted to pluck
it out. This, again, would be work, and
sinful. Healing also was work. An in-

jured man might apply a bandage to his wound on the sabbath provided that the bandage was intended only to prevent the wound from growing worse. If, however, the bandage was employed to effect a cure —if, for instance, it contained any remedial ointment—then its application on a sabbath was a heinous sin.

Such inept sophistries, as St. Mark records, stirred Jesus to "anger." He exposed their falsity with remorseless logic. By appeals to common-sense he proved that it was "lawful" to do good on the sabbath day. He demolished the whole cumbrous mass of tradition by his incontestable principle that the sabbath was made for man, not man for the sabbath. Yet no verbal argument, however convincing, could proclaim his doctrine so forcibly as could action. Therefore he taught by deed also what his views were. In the synagogue on a sabbath day was a man with a withered hand. In the sight of all the people Jesus healed him.

Thereby he put his own views beyond question, and illustrated them in a way which none could disregard.

Soon he made his works of healing an essential part of his ministry. They were far more than incidental works of compassion. They were a designed part of his teaching; the healing and the preaching were closely linked. The Matthæan Gospel thus summarizes the work in Galilee: "He went about all the cities and villages, teaching in their synagogues, and preaching the gospel of the kingdom, and healing all manner of disease and all manner of sickness." Later, Jesus committed the same dual ministry to his apostles. In St. Luke's words, "he gave them power and authority over all devils and to cure diseases. And he sent them forth to preach the kingdom of God, and to heal the sick." We may ask why Jesus attached so evident an importance to this work of healing. In part, no doubt, he did it from simple compassion for human suffering. He could not look unmoved on misery; he rejoiced to bestow happiness.

Yet by itself this explanation does not seem adequate. There must have been further reasons for placing the work of healing on the same rank as the work of preaching. Its results were necessarily transient, for those whom Jesus cured must again, sooner or later, fall ill, and suffer, and die. Yet, in another sense, its influence was to endure. Apart from the temporary relief given to the sick, it contributed to the permanent legacy of teaching, and chiefly by establishing the spiritual authority of the teacher. There was a day when Jesus had said to a paralytic, "thy sins be forgiven thee," and some of the bystanders, naturally enough, questioned his right to use these astounding words. But Jesus promptly justified his claim to heal the soul by demonstrating his power to cure the body: "That ye may know that the Son of man hath power on earth

to forgive sins," he said, " arise, and take
up thy bed, and go unto thy house." No
other demonstration could have been so
swiftly convincing. " Amazement took
hold on all," comments the evangelist,
" and they glorified God; and they were
filled with fear, saying, We have seen
strange things to-day."

Thus the works of healing were teaching
by deed. Power shown in the material and
visible region of life made easier belief
concerning power in the spiritual and
invisible region of the soul.

III

And the unseen world, as the Jews of this
age conceived it, included armies of spirits,
both good and evil. To the evil spirits,
led by Beelzebub, were attributed insanity,
epilepsy, and various other maladies. To
effect a cure, therefore, it was necessary to
" cast out " the evil spirit. Jesus himself
had been educated in that belief, and there

is no sign that he ever abandoned it. Indeed, there are still bewildering cases for which some alienists and psychologists would admit that the theory of "demoniacal possession" is at least as good an explanation as any other. In any event, moreover, it would have been contrary to the methods of Jesus had he diverted attention from his real purpose by attempting to recast the medical knowledge of his day. Ever he sought to concentrate attention on the essential truths he had come to proclaim. But, accepting the theory of evil spirits, he used it as a chance of showing that the divine power flowing through him could conquer evil. His opponents, unable to deny the cures he wrought, fell back upon the plea that he cast out devils "by Beelzebub, the chief of the devils." With swift logic Jesus demolished that argument. Evil would not cast out evil, else would it be a kingdom divided against itself, which could not stand. "But if I by the spirit of God cast out devils, then is the kingdom of God come upon you." These words help us again to realize that this exorcism of evil spirits was not only a work of compassion but a designed and definite part of the teaching. As Jesus came to each town or village, by word he proclaimed " the kingdom of God "; by deed he showed that " the kingdom of God is come upon you."

In yet another way, we may believe, the works of healing were employed to illustrate visibly a point of doctrine. There was— and, indeed, there is still—a view which attempted to solve the problem of physical evil by accepting disease as an ordinance of God, meant to serve as a punishment for sin or as a wholesome discipline. That view, we shall remember, is the theme debated in the noble drama of the Book of Job. Jesus did not concern himself with any abstract discussion of the problem, a discussion which could only have bemused his simple hearers. When the disciples asked, " Rabbi, who did sin, this man or

his parents, that he was born blind?"
Jesus was content to answer, "Neither did
this man sin nor his parents, but that the
works of God should be made manifest in
him"—and therewith gave the blind man
sight. Then only was the man as God
meant him, was God's handiwork recog-
nizable in him. In certain instances Jesus
recognized that sin and suffering were
closely linked as cause and effect, when
"go, and sin no more" would be his word
to the healed. But sin and suffering alike
were foreign to God's design, and against
both, by word and deed, he waged incessant
war. Preaching and healing, and by both
these means teaching, Jesus journeyed
through Galilee.

Not only did he combat resolutely both
disease and sin, but—a fact yet more
significant—he viewed sin as he viewed
disease. He hated its foulness. But he
regarded it as something extrinsic to man,
something that, like disease, had thrust
itself in and made havoc of God's design.

Just as the normal man should be the man healthy in body, so the normal man was he whose will, strengthened by divine power, should be immune against the attempted dominance of moral ill. The good man was not man changed into a being abnormal and inhuman; the good man was the true man, the man himself cleansed from what was foreign to his best nature. That was the source of his unconquerable optimism about characters which others thought hopelessly degraded. That was why no moral failure on the part of his friends could ever make him despair of them. That was why to a group of very ordinary folk, acutely conscious of the gulf between the ideals he pictured and their own ways of living, he could give with tranquil confidence the amazing command, " Be ye perfect, even as your Father in heaven is perfect."

Again he enforced this doctrine by deed as well as by word. In Palestine were some people adjudged by all respectable folk to

be quite beyond the pale; moral and social
outcasts with whom no self-respecting Jew
could be on terms of friendship. Such were
the "publicans," men employed by the
Roman government to collect the customs
on exports levied in the province of Palestine. The system under which they worked
encouraged dishonesty. Often the publican
paid down a fixed sum to Rome for his
tenure of office, and then proceeded to
reimburse himself, with something over, by
the sums he collected. By false representa-
tions, threats, and blackmail it would be
easy for him to exact from uneducated
people amounts far in excess of those for
which they were liable under the legal rates
of tariff. But even if he fulfilled its duties
with comparative honesty, the very office
which a publican held earned him the contempt and hatred of his fellow-countrymen.
That a Jew for the sake of lucre should
assist in collecting the revenue demanded
by the abominated power of Rome seemed
insufferable. Hence as a rule the only

persons willing to undertake this detested work were men of no character, who already had been in trouble and therefore found themselves unable to get other employment. The publican, in short, was deemed a traitor to his nation and his religion.

Not less contemptible, in the accepted view, were the folk known as "sinners." They were men and women who had abandoned their places among God's chosen people, mixing with Gentiles and eating their food, taking no part in public worship and openly defying the Law. They formed a kind of underworld, and among them were many women who lived on the wages of immorality.

Probably nothing that Jesus said and did so staggered the religious people of his day as his attitude towards these classes, the publicans and the "sinners." He came before the people of his time, it must be remembered, as a rabbi. He was accepted as one of their authorized religious teachers, whose main task was to uphold and expound the Law. When he began a story about a Pharisee and a publican, the listeners would nod approvingly. They knew well both types; the Pharisee—the man " separated," as the name means, from the crowd by his superior " righteousness," by his punctilious observance of the Law; and the publican, the irreligious and unpatriotic renegade. Conceive, then, the limitless astonishment at the ending of the story, at the emphatic declaration that the publican was justified rather than the Pharisee !

But the deeds were as startling and as decisive as the words. Of the men whom Jesus chose to be his closest companions, one was a publican. Then he became this man's guest, " and it came to pass that he was sitting at meat in his house, and many publicans and sinners sat down with Jesus and his disciples." The ordinary religious-minded Jew, though he was no Pharisee or rigorist, would be aghast at the idea of eating with publicans and sinners. In this striking and dramatic way, more vividly

even than by his words, Jesus insisted that
the kingdom he proclaimed was open to
all, and that his appeal was more likely to
reach the "sinners" who desired amend-
ment and a real religion than the self-
satisfied "righteous," content with mere
external obedience to a code. But the
spectacle of a rabbi not merely deign-
ing to speak, but sitting at table, with
publicans and sinners, was not less than
astounding.

Equally significant, and equally uncon-
ventional, was the attitude of Jesus on
another occasion, most vividly pictured by
St. Luke. On this day, by way of contrast,
Jesus was the guest, not of a publican, but
of a Pharisee. Yet this Pharisee had
omitted those acts of courtesy which were
due to a guest on his arrival. Then, as
they reclined at meat, "a woman which was
in the city, a sinner," stole in through the
open door. She must have listened to
Jesus as he taught in Capernaum; likely
enough, he had spoken to her apart, had

H

urged her to quit her miserable trade. She
had listened yearning, yet reluctant; and,
at the last, had turned away to brood over
his haunting words. And now her decision
is made. Hearing that he is dining with
Simon the Pharisee, she creeps in, un-
noticed by the slaves. She carries an
alabaster phial of perfume—a part, perhaps, of her tragic earnings, the gift of one
of her so many lovers. In a moment,
before any has realized her presence, she
is at the feet of Jesus, whom she sees dimly
through her tears. Her hands go swiftly to
her head; it is held by the Jews a shameful
thing that a woman should let down her
hair in public; but what does she care for
that? And then, " weeping, she began to
wet his feet with her tears, and wiped them
with the hair of her head, and kissed his
feet, and anointed them." The company
were aghast. The host said nothing, but
his face revealed his thought : " This man,
if he were a prophet, would have perceived
who and what manner of woman this is

which toucheth him, that she is a sinner."
It is needless to re-tell at length the rest of
the familiar story—the rebuke, as delicate
as unanswerable, given to the Pharisee, the
word pardoning the " many sins " of the
woman, " for she loved much "—whereat
the guests whispered, " Who is this that even
forgiveth sins ? "—and the heartening fare-
well which bade her enter into peace. It is
one of those scenes—and the Gospels
abound with them—which scarcely the
greatest literary genius could have invented,
or, having invented, could have told with
such vivid simplicity. But the point which
concerns us here is to note how the deeds
of Jesus helped the words to set forth his
teaching, and how startling to the thought
of his age his doctrine was. It was not the
product of evolution. It was not a purified
or humanized Judaism, a Judaism reaching
a higher standard than any previously
attained. It was wholly different. It was,
to repeat once more that pregnant comment
of its first hearers, " a new teaching."

IV

When we are considering the teaching given by deed, our minds are apt to turn specially to those acts of supra-normal power commonly known as " miracles." Yet it is easy to place too great emphasis upon them, or at least emphasis of a mistaken kind. It is true that they form an integral part of the Gospels, being so woven into the text that any effort to separate them, and to conceive the miracles as interpolations of later times, proves hopelessly impossible. Beyond all question, the first three Gospels were written within the lifetime of many who had witnessed the events described, and it is noteworthy that miracles are far more numerous in the first three than they are in the Fourth Gospel, the publication of which belongs to a much later date. Again, if any reader will study the earliest Gospel, that of St. Mark, and then face the suggestion that all the supranormal works, done on the scale and with the publicity there described, were simply imagined by the disciples, and that nothing like them ever happened, he will quickly feel that such a theory involves difficulties greater than those it is intended to remove.

On the other hand, we cannot but notice how fully the use made by Jesus of supra-normal powers accords with the decisions to which he won through in the wilderness. Jesus will never use these powers for his own glory, or for the sake of making a sensation. He refuses entirely to employ them when challenged by curious sight-seers. Of some thirty-five miracles [1] separately recorded in the Gospels, no fewer than twenty-eight are works of heal-ing. To these must be added a vast number of others, not separately specified, but collectively included in such a state-ment as that, journeying through a certain

[1] The number cannot be given with precision, because it is occasionally uncertain whether two stories in two Gospels describe separate incidents, or whether they describe the same incident with some slight differences of setting or detail.

district, he " healed all manner of diseases."
Probably we may assume safely that nine-
tenths at least of the " miracles " were
deeds of healing. Of the few others that
are described, most were worked to meet
some special need, such as the feeding of a
hungry multitude, or the stilling of a storm
at a moment of acute danger. We have
noted already how quietly, yet effectively,
the miracles were used to illustrate and
enforce the teaching. They seem, if the
word be allowed, to come naturally from
Jesus. They are as different as possible
from spectacular deeds such as imagination
might have attributed to him.

Yet unquestionably they imply the possession of supra-normal powers. Some of
the works of healing can be assigned to
psycho-therapeutic means which we need
no longer view as miraculous. But this
cannot be said of all, such as the cleansing
from leprosy, or, again, of other miracles
such as the stilling of a storm. Not one
was " contrary to nature," unless we in-

terpret nature in terms of purely mechanical causation. The miracles do imply, however, knowledge, and consequent powers, more than normal man has yet attained, or the interaction of the spiritual factor in ways beyond our present understanding.

But when all has been said—and there is material here, of course, not merely for a few lines of summary, but for volumes of abstruse discussion—we may repeat that this question of the miracles is often given a wrong importance, because it is seen in a wrong perspective. There are people who suppose the Gospels would be easier to accept were the supernatural element omitted from them. There are people who declare that they " believe in Jesus," yet doubt if they can " believe the stories of miracles." So they examine them again, and argue about evidence, and causation, and " fixed laws of nature," probably finding themselves at the end in a rather dense fog. Well, that is inevitable. They have taken a wrong line. It is futile to attempt first to decide, as a separate issue, the question of the Gospel miracles, and thence to go on to consider belief in Jesus. That is to put things in their wrong order. If any reader of this page feels perplexed by this question of the miracles, here is the right course for him to take. Let him deliberately put that question aside for the present. It will answer itself later, and, relatively, it is quite unimportant. It is not what we believe about miracles that matters, but what we believe about Jesus. If we believe that Jesus was what he claimed to be, there will be little difficulty about the miracles. For instance, was a storm on the Sea of Galilee suddenly ended by natural causes, or by a spoken word? The answer depends, not on what we believe about storms, but on what we believe about him who was in the boat with his disciples.

His claims were explicit. They were not put into his mouth by later ages. In the first-written of the Gospels we find him confronted by Caiaphas's direct challenge :

"Art thou the Christ, the Son of the Blessed?" And Jesus said, "I am." Was that overwhelming assertion true? If it was not true, the speaker was either an impostor or a self-deluded fanatic. If it was true, what cause have we to hesitate over the record that his word could end a storm? What might seem incredible would be the Christ with no powers transcending those of a merely human being. If that "I am" is false, then all Christianity is false. If that "I am" is true, then to stumble over stories of miracles, all less miraculous than himself, seems needless indeed. "Whom say ye that I am?" All turns on that. In order to reach a reasoned answer to the supreme question, it is worth while to study dispassionately again and again, as we are attempting to do in these pages, the evidence before us, the main incidents of his life, its setting, its character, its impression upon those who witnessed it. Because that enquiry transcends in importance—and, in a sense includes—all else, it would be unwise to turn aside from it in order to discuss at greater length the credibility of the " miracles."

V

We have seen, then, Jesus travelling through the northern province of Galilee as a rabbi, teaching in each place he visited, both by word and deed. We have seen that in its early stages his ministry was enormously successful. But in time there came a change. Opposition began to show itself, at first local and occasional in character, but afterwards definitely organized. Other teachers of religion observed with dismay the vast crowds that followed Jesus and his increasing influence upon them. Reports of the strange scenes witnessed and of the subversive doctrines which this rabbi was encouraging perturbed not merely the scribes attached to the synagogues of Galilee but both Pharisees and Sadducees in Jerusalem itself. More than once they sent agents into the north country with instructions to bring back full reports about this new teacher, and his alleged popularity, and the nature of his instruction.

The unworthy motive of jealousy, powerful though it was, did not stand alone in causing opposition to Jesus. The news of his teaching, and most of all his teaching by deed, must have caused quite genuine pain and resentment among many of the most pious and educated people of the day. Unsatisfying as they must have felt legalism to be as a substitute for personal religion, they were fully convinced that it had divine sanction. They were sure, for instance, that to break the traditional rules about the sabbath was to offend God. Those who had come under the direct influence of Jesus, those who had heard his actual words and seen him face to face, had mostly found reason to change their views. Others, however, knew only by hearsay how, rabbi though he was, he had defied what they accounted among the fundamental and most sacred rules of religion. We cannot wonder that they were scandalized. Other Jews, probably, were offended for reasons of a different kind. These were not particularly religious people. They were not greatly concerned whatever new teaching some new rabbi might give. Yet the line, they felt, must be drawn somewhere. And when a rabbi so far forgot what was due to his race and himself as to sit down at table with publicans and sinners, then it was high time for a protest to be made.

Feelings of that kind among the governing religious and social classes were bound to have their effect. Among the earliest results was the exclusion of Jesus from the synagogues. At first the rulers of these places had treated him with the deference due to a well-known rabbi, and had invited him to preach at the sabbath-day services. Now this opportunity was withheld, and all the teaching had to be given in private houses or in the open air. Another result was that the leading people began to feel nervous about seeming to sympathize with a teacher whom the Pharisees and Sadducees had denounced. Consequently, they were more loth than they had been to show hospitality to Jesus and his companions, so that at least once Jesus " had not where to lay his head."

In addition to incurring the enmity of religious leaders and the suspicion of those whom such leaders influenced, Jesus found himself, as time went on, in increasing danger of political attack. He was in the territory of Herod Antipas, who had imprisoned the Baptist, and afterwards beheaded him. He and his advisers were greatly perturbed by the rumours that came to them of Jesus and his teaching. This talk of a " kingdom of God " seemed like the language of a revolutionary plotting against the rule of Herod. Moreover, after John's death there were stories that he had risen again in the person of Jesus, and the conscience of Antipas was ill at ease. Thus Jesus was increasingly in danger of

arrest.   Already the political and religious
factions were ready to make common cause
against him.   When he wrought one of his
first deeds of healing on a sabbath, the
Pharisees who watched it "went out and
straightway with the Herodians took counsel against him, how they might destroy
him."

Through such causes the conditions in
which Jesus worked in Galilee became less
favourable.   It is true that wherever he
taught, great multitudes still flocked to
hear him.   Deep was his love for them,
and staunch their loyalty to him.   Yet
the very size of these crowds and their
ardour often became an embarrassment.
There were moments when he had to risk
losing all their favour, because he disappointed them by refusing to proclaim
himself the Christ, and would not head the
national movement for which they looked.
He had to resist forcible attempts to make
him their king.   Again, the crowds made
it most difficult for him to secure those

seasons of repose and solitude and prayer
which he found essential. Above all, it was
impossible to be sure of any permanence
for teaching given to varying multitudes.
Jesus was, as he himself said, like a sower
scattering seed broadcast, and but a very
small proportion of it fell on good ground.
Many listened from mere curiosity. Many
understood little or nothing of the deeper
meaning in what they heard. Many who
understood something were influenced by
it for a short time only. In view of these
facts, Jesus had to reconsider his methods.
The outward conditions had changed.
Galilee was no longer a province in which
he could work with security. So far, he
had left it, since the beginning of his
ministry, only to attend periodically the
great religious festivals in Jerusalem. But
now he must be ready for sudden and
forced retreats from it when the plots of
his enemies became actively threatening.

Again, how was the effect of his teaching
to be made permanent? How was its

transmission still to be secured if, as the fate of the Baptist and the attitude of Herod made too probable, Jesus himself should be arrested?

Here, then, was a new situation. Here were new dangers. Here were new problems. With serene wisdom Jesus set himself to meet them.

CHAPTER V

THE TEACHING BY CHARACTER

I

THE teaching of Jesus has two contrasting characteristics, of which its timeliness is one and its timelessness the other. In a sense it belongs, as we should expect, to a special age. It reflects the conditions and knowledge of that age. It is not abstract philosophy, spoken into space, but practical counsel given to men and women among whom the teacher lived. It abounds with homely illustrations drawn from their everyday affairs. There is a sense, then, in which it is vividly of the moment.

Yet, side by side with this, we find the other quality of permanence. Jesus seems to be conscious that he is addressing, not merely those about him, but the people of all future ages. "Heaven and earth shall pass away," he declares, "but my words shall not pass away." Repeatedly what he says is shaped by the conviction that it will be eagerly consulted for guidance in far distant times. He is asked, for instance, some question that has arisen out of a trivial controversy of the day—perhaps a squabble between two brothers over an inheritance. He could answer in a way that would deal with that special case on its merits and serve well enough to end the dispute. Instead, he deals, not merely with the special case, but with large principles beneath it, and so gives teaching of abiding validity.

How, then, could he secure permanence for his message? At first he may have hoped for its acceptance by the official leaders of religion. But their jealous hostility soon showed that their one aim would be to discredit and suppress what Jesus taught. They clung to the political idea of the promised kingdom. The Sadducees adhered to belief in God as a deity who must be propitiated by sacrifices. Their chief concern was to uphold the Temple and its system of worship, from which they derived power and wealth. The Pharisees would not modify their doctrine that righteousness began and ended with obedience to the Law as expanded by tradition. Jesus, on the other hand, interpreted God in terms of Fatherhood, interpreted the Kingdom in terms of faith and hope, interpreted the Law in terms of love. How was this Gospel to be spread? He knew that his personal ministry was precarious. There was a real risk that Herod's emissaries would arrest him and cut short his work. But, beyond that, lurked a more certain danger. The time would come when he must publicly proclaim himself the Messiah. Only too well he knew that this would intensify the bitterness of the official religious leaders against him. Inevitably also it must damp the enthusiasm of those who had persisted in thinking that, sooner or later, he would give the signal for political revolt. Jesus was under no illusion; throughout he saw plainly that his announcement of Messiahship must doom him to death.

What chance would his teaching then have of survival? Individuals from the crowds might cherish and repeat such parts of it as they had heard, and those disciples who had journeyed with him from place to place would have a fuller store of memories. But there had been no chance as yet of giving even the disciples adequate instruction. They were a large and changing body, some of whom had been compelled to return to their ordinary work, and some after a while had taken offence at his doctrine, and " walked no more with him." The most he could hope was that for a time fragments of his message, imperfectly understood, would be preserved. As the years went on, their force would dwindle, and his teaching, both by word and deed,

would linger as little more than a vague
memory.

As ever when he had to make decisions
of great importance, Jesus went apart for
solitary prayer, and thus thought out the
course he should take.   He had returned
to Capernaum, and wandered alone into the
hill country behind the town.   " He went
out into the mountain to pray," St. Luke
writes, " and he continued all night in
prayer to God."   Nothing less than the
whole future of his Gospel was at stake.
When the morning came, his resolve was
formed.   From the large company of disciples he would summon twelve ; " whom
he himself would," in St. Mark's phrase,
" that they might be with him and that
he might send them forth to preach."
Henceforward he would concentrate upon
teaching and training these twelve.   When
occasion served, he would still welcome the
multitudes, and speak in their hearing words
of counsel and warning and encouragement.

Yet this would be no longer his chief task. In place of teaching a great many people a little, he would devote himself to teaching a few people a great deal. Yet always he would cause them to regard what they learnt, not as an esoteric secret, given for their own learning and profit alone, but as a message committed to them in order that later they might transmit it to others. This little group was to form the nucleus of a society, intended ultimately to include Jew and Gentile alike. Within this society could be practised those virtues of love and service which lay near the basis of his creed. Its members would help and reinforce one another. They would embody, as it were, his doctrine of a spiritual kingdom. Very soon he would send out the twelve to preach and minister. Thus from the beginning they would be guarded against imagining wrongly that what they heard was to remain their own secret. Thus, too, they would have practice in the work while it was still possible for them to come back and "tell him all things, both what they had done and what they had taught." So they would be trained to carry on his work in years to come, when he was no longer to be seen among them. From them, too, others would learn to teach, and thus the perpetuation of his message would be secured.

II

Because so much depended on them, we cannot doubt that the choice of the twelve was made with most deliberate care. Among them were the four fishermen who probably accompanied Jesus when he joined the Baptist, and remained for some time among the disciples of John. But it is not easy to find any one quality, beyond a common love of the master and a common willingness to learn from him, distinguishing all the twelve. Rather it seems that they were chosen for their diversity, and as if Jesus wished to demonstrate that no special temperament or type of character was needed for those who were to be his followers. The eminently sane man of affairs, the pessimist, the quick-tempered and impulsive man, the thoughtful and contemplative man—such were some of the twelve. They included also an ex-publican, the professional agent of the Roman government, and an ex-"zealot," a member, that is, of an organization sworn to overthrow the Roman rule. This (to take an analogy from modern times) was much as though an Orangeman and a Sinn Feiner had been brought into close companionship. That both Matthew the publican and Simon the Zealot were of the twelve is a fact which helps us to realize the compelling power of Jesus.

Finally, we may suppose he wished to show that this chosen company was not limited to those who, like himself, were Galilæans. Therefore he took one of the twelve from southern Palestine. This was Judas *ish-Kerioth*, or " Iscariot," which means " a man of Kerioth," in Judæa. It was like joining one Devonian with eleven

Yorkshiremen. A bold experiment; was there from the first some lack of sympathy between the eleven and the one? Yet the venture was deliberate, and made, we may suppose, because Jesus discerned in Iscariot great possibilities of good and also of evil. To keep this man near himself and to give him a new sense of responsibility as one of the twelve was to provide him with his best chance. A venture, certainly, but a venture which might save a soul, and from a venture which might do that it was not the habit of Jesus to shrink. For a time, too, it seemed successful; we should remember that Judas, like the other apostles, was sent forth to preach and cast out devils, and did so with marked effect, and returned " with great joy."

This striking and decisive step, the appointment of the twelve apostles, had at least one result beyond those we have noticed already. It enabled Jesus the teacher to develop his teaching in a new way. Living more apart from the multi-

tudes than he had done, concentrating his
attention upon the training of the twelve,
he would continue to teach them, as he had
taught the larger body of disciples and the
mixed crowds who gathered about him,
both by word and by deed. But, in addition to those means of instruction, his new
manner of life enabled him fully to employ
for the first time another means, in a sense
the most powerful of all. Living daily in
intimate companionship with the twelve,
he taught them, not only by word and deed,
but by character. We may even say that
he taught them less by what he did and
said than by what he was. No doubt his
wonderful personality had impressed even
casual listeners, and helped to gain an eager
audience for his doctrine. Yet such a
glimpse of it, or even the fuller knowledge
that came to the general company of disciples, could not approach the revelation
bestowed on this little group of private
friends. It was much to hear, as they
alone heard, the Teacher's own explanation

of his parables. It was much to see, as
they alone saw, some of his most striking
and significant actions. But it was more
to be with him, day after day, to be given
his confidence, to watch, in every change
of circumstance, his unchanging self. And
what they learnt in this way was also to be
a part of the message which afterwards
they were to transmit to the world at large.

III

What, we may ask, were the characteristics of Jesus which specially impressed
these men who saw him daily, at close
range? We can derive our answers from
the records which they bequeathed, for
these were embodied later in the written
Gospels which have come down to us. And
first, beyond question, was the unstained
holiness of their master. It was not merely
a public view that they had of him. They
saw him in the intimate little affairs of life,
they saw him when things went wrong in

an irritating fashion, they "continued with
him," as he himself testified, "in his
temptations"—not merely crucial moments
of great trial, but the lesser temptations of
ordinary life. And never once did his
practice fall below his precept. Like Pilate,
though in a sense far wider, those who were
with him continually could "find no fault
in this man." Of any other it may be said
that in proportion with moral growth
grows the sense of imperfection, and of the
need of asking forgiveness. Yet Jesus,
praying often that others might be forgiven, and commending those who so
prayed, was never heard to ask forgiveness
for himself. Never had he to lament anything done amiss or any opportunity unused
as he looked back on his life. And the
teaching given thus by character made
luminous the teaching by word. All the
hearers, accustomed to the traditional interpretation of "righteousness," were astounded when Jesus told them that they
could not enter the kingdom of heaven

unless their righteousness exceeded that of the Pharisees—for the Pharisees, punctiliously observing the traditions, alone attained righteousness as the Jews understood it. To exceed their righteousness seemed impracticable indeed. But then the flawless character of Jesus demonstrated what righteousness meant as he used the word, and for the apostles this new meaning swept away the old.

This holiness, this absolute purity of their master, filled the twelve with a sense of awe. Easy and intimate as was much of their conversation with him, there were moments when they were almost overwhelmed by the consciousness of supernatural power. That was the feeling which expressed itself instinctively in Peter's cry, " Depart from me, for I am a sinful man, O Lord ! " And that was the feeling which made them accept without demur the amazing personal claims inherent in the teaching of Jesus. Apart from his unique character, they would have seemed, in some instances, intolerably arrogant, and, in others, the language of dementia. Our own familiarity with them may easily make us forget what they involve. They do not consist of a few exceptional words spoken in some passing mood of exaltation. They are not an occasional sentence which could have been interpolated in the Gospels, nor, indeed, are they such as anyone could have imagined. They are tranquil sayings pervading the Gospels throughout, and they form the basis on which the entire teaching of Jesus stands. If on such a point we distrust, as of comparatively late date, the evidence of the Fourth Gospel, we can find words startling enough on almost every page of the earlier three. Jesus sweeps aside the whole religious system of his age with no argument beyond a mere " but I say unto you." To be like one whose house is built on a rock, he adds, a man must hear and obey his words. He claims the power to forgive sins. He says of himself that one greater than Solomon or Jonah is here. He bids the weary at heart, not to turn to God, but to " come unto me, and I will give you rest." He states that " he that loveth father or mother more than me is not worthy of me." He promises to all who have left kindred or possessions for his sake an hundredfold more in this world, " and in the world to come life everlasting." He says that all power has been given to him, " in heaven and on earth."

The real character of such utterances— and many more examples from the first three Gospels could be added—must be faced. Was their speaker no more than a wonderfully good man? On the contrary, any mere man who had spoken them would not deserve to be called good. He would have been a grotesque egotist, of whom it would be charitable to suppose that he had lost his reason. Yet the words come from Jesus with a calm inevitableness. It is idle to admire the " beauty of his moral teaching " and to ignore these staggering claims, for the claims are an integral part of the teaching, are indeed the primary assumptions on which it is based. And they who listened felt that even the loftiest of such claims fell naturally from the lips of Jesus. For all their marvel, there seemed no incongruity between his language and his character. We cannot wonder that an increasing sense of awe possessed the apostles as, day by day, they listened to the serene teaching of their master. Who in truth was he? So the doubtful whispers began to pass from one to another. They had fancied they knew all about him. He was Jesus of Nazareth, an ex-carpenter who had taken up the profession of a rabbi. He was a most attractive if bewildering teacher. He was a wonderfully sympathetic friend. He had a surprising knowledge of human nature. He could work marvellous cures.

Yes, but any such account of him no longer sufficed. Intimacy is apt to lessen the sense of awe, but they found that the longer they lived with Jesus the more this sense of awe increased. Jesus of Nazareth

—yes, but what else? The promised Christ? He had refused to come forward as the Messiah, and fled from the crowds who would have forced him into leadership. And yet. . . . There were times when Jesus withdrew himself from the twelve for solitary thought and prayer. Then we can imagine how eagerly they discussed this question among themselves, how different would be the answers of Peter and Thomas, how John would brood much but say little; how suddenly the hot debate would be hushed as the returning figure of Jesus was discerned. Day by day, though, they were being taught by his character, that character of which his words, even the most stupendous, were no more than the direct and undistorting expression.

Apart from this supernatural holiness and authority, there were qualities in Jesus which must have impressed deeply these men living in close companionship with him. Such, for example, was his courage. No threats and no adverse circumstances could

K

divert him from his purpose. Again, it would have been easy for him, and many would have deemed it an act of wise prudence, to conciliate the civil and ecclesiastical authorities. The chances of his success as a preacher would have greatly increased, from the world's point of view, had he at least abstained from denouncing the powerful Pharisees and the wealthy Sadducees. Yet he who showed himself so gentle and compassionate to the humblest or most sin-stained of the folk who sought his aid, would make not the slightest compromise with the impenitent in high places, could speak the most scathing denunciation the world has ever heard. He was wholly without fear. And though his heart was wrung often by the ingratitude and faithlessness of those for whom he laboured, though there must have been dark seasons when the temptation to abandon his task was strong, in all such tests his courage brought him through triumphantly.

IV

Closely linked with this courage was his optimism. This was derived from an absolute faith in his heavenly Father, and a complete certainty about the Father's power and love. The simple folk who lived with Jesus were not of a kind to indulge in philosophical speculations. Yet they, like all other human beings, had to face at times the great problems of existence. Jesus himself was brought into touch with such problems by daily experience. An optimistic view of life may be attained not seldom by those who themselves are sheltered, have little cause for anxiety, and are rarely in touch with the more grim and sordid aspects of human existence. But the life of Jesus was spent in very different circumstances. His own fierce conflicts with temptation, and his knowledge of the havoc wrought in the world by sin, constrained him to face the

problem of moral evil. With physical evil,
often in its most loathsome forms, he was
brought into touch constantly, as he set
himself to heal the sick, as a concourse of
marred and agonized sufferers awaited him
in each place he visited.

Yet for him—and the fact is of immeasur-
able significance—all the world seemed
radiant with the Father's love. He found
evidence of it throughout the countryside;
the birds and the flowers sang this message
to him. Not the suffering he had to
witness, or that, of body and mind, which
he himself had to undergo, or the warfare
in the natural world, could dim his certainty. This was for him not a matter for
argument, but the primary fact of existence,
a fact so plain that he marvelled at the
blindness of those who failed to discern it
—this fact that God is a Father who cares
in tender love for all that he has made, who
hears all prayer, who supplies all need.
And always to his companions the character
of Jesus, with its utter consecration to

doing the Father's will, must have confirmed his doctrine of the Fatherhood.

Again, they needs must have been impressed by his optimism concerning man. He knew, they admitted, what was in man. He knew man's weakness, mixed motives, gross desires. He knew what human cruelty and baseness could accomplish. He knew, and was saddened by the knowledge, how inconstant had proved many who for a time had walked as his disciples. Yet his belief in man's possibilities was unshaken. He had shown it afresh by entrusting the future of his Gospel to the twelve. He had welcomed as friends many whom the respectable opinion of his time would not even recognize as acquaintances. In after years, when the apostles had themselves to work among people of all conditions, we may surmise how often intolerance was checked and charity made easier through a remembrance of the lessons taught them by the character of Jesus.

This optimism concerning God and man

brought him a serene composure, a detachment from ordinary cares which to his close friends must have been one of the strongest, as it was among the most surprising, features of his character. It was a new kind of detachment. It had little in common with asceticism. The Baptist, to take an obvious contrast, had deliberately cut himself off from the normal pleasures and solaces of human existence. He was an ascetic in dress, in habits, in food. But Jesus was no ascetic; indeed, his frank enjoyment of social pleasures caused his enemies to traduce him as "a gluttonous man and a wine-bibber." He preached no social revolution. Men who were rich and used their possessions wisely he praised. Riches were of no importance in themselves, but they provided a test of character, and those who were remiss in their use of even "that which is least" were scarcely fit to be entrusted with "the true riches." Men who were enslaved by their riches he blamed and warned. They were imperilling their souls, and what should a man give in exchange for his soul? The man who was mastered by worldly possessions, instead of being their master, would be wise to cut himself free from this bondage at all costs, and to part with everything he had. The poor were happy in being exempt from the temptations of wealth, the power of which Jesus recognized. Too often they thwarted the growth of that type of character which could find a place in the divine kingdom. Yet such dangers could be overcome; with God's help all things were possible.

In themselves, then, according to this view, riches simply did not matter. Their effect upon character must be watched, for character mattered supremely. Otherwise they, and all such material things, were unimportant. If they were given, let them be used well or renounced. If they were withheld, let not their absence be deplored. These were not the things in life that counted for much, one way or another.

" Happy are the detached," said Jesus—
such seems to be the force of the phrase
" poor in spirit "—and he set forth this
virtue of detachment by example. His
companions must have been continually
impressed and taught by his serene composure. He was never " anxious for the
morrow." Equably he took things as they
came. He did not despise either material
comfort or social happiness; he was willing
enough to be a guest at a wedding or a
dinner. But when his popularity with the
well-to-do waned, when he had to undergo
hardship, and often was in personal danger,
he was by no means discomfited. He was
gloriously detached, and exempt from those
haunting worries which do so much to
make many human lives ineffective.

If such an attitude was not gained by
asceticism, still less was it due to indifference. No sympathies were so alert as
those of Jesus, none were more acutely
conscious of the mingled joys and sorrows
of life. His detachment from much that

most people think of primary importance sprang from the fact that he himself held, and tried to impress upon his disciples, a new set of values. It was not easy to make others accept them. His adherence to them vastly increased the difficulty of his work. Even now, perhaps, we have not adopted that scale of values for our own normal use. It regarded life from a new point of view, and ranged its details in a new order of importance. That, for instance, which the Pharisees accounted extreme righteousness, was not held by Jesus to be of any worth in God's sight, while he treated as venial some sins which they deemed beyond pardon. All existence he interpreted in terms of spiritual, not physical, life; all duty he saw in a new sense as the loving service of God and man. What men termed death was but an incident in the unbroken life. The only death to be feared was the death of the soul, and against this all who set themselves resolutely to obey his teaching would be made immune. He had come to lead man into this true life, a life of which the test was not a beating heart but a will pulsing in tune with the will of God.

"A new teaching" indeed! We set it beside the arid creed of legalism, which all the Jews of this period had been taught from their earliest years. And so we realize better the immense task of Jesus in trying to make a group of quite ordinary folk conversant with the truths he revealed, and to give them so clear a grasp that they would be able to transmit them faithfully and fully to others. Upon this task he spent unfaltering labour. His instruction of casual multitudes now became infrequent and incidental. He must concentrate on training the twelve he had chosen, in order that through them his message might be perpetuated. And, short as the time would be, he must use infinite patience. Often enough they seemed exasperatingly dense. But he taught them "as they were able to

bear it," enforcing one lesson at a time.
So, day after day, the work went on. He
taught by word, by question and answer,
by parables and explanations of parables.
We possess, of course, but a small proportion of the lessons he spoke to the apostles.
Their training went on as they walked along
the road, or rested by the wayside, or, when
the chill night fell, gathered round the fire
for their simple meal. We cannot doubt
that, like other rabbis, and as they would
expect, he made them repeat after him
some of his terse and vivid sayings until
they had them by heart. They made
request for that method when they said
" teach us to pray," and, sentence by
sentence, they learnt the pattern prayer.

He taught them, as he had taught the
crowds, by deed also. For instance, he
had spoken often of the duty of service.
Not all his words, perhaps, would they keep
faithfully in their memories. But never
could they forget the deed which translated

precepts into action. Never could they forget that scene when, towards the close of his ministry, he fulfilled for them the duties of a slave, and knelt before them all in turn, and washed their feet. "I have given you an example," he said, "that ye also should do as I have done to you."

Yet, even more than by word or deed, he taught them by his character. He had called the twelve, to quote again St. Mark's words, "that they might be with him and that he might send them forth to preach." To be with him was the first stage. Only by being with him could they learn their message. For that message was ultimately to have as its centre, not ethical or moral counsel, but himself. He was to be the theme they would set before the world. And the whole validity of the new doctrine must depend, as we have seen, upon the belief about him who gave it. Keenly as he realized this, Jesus would make no effort to force belief about himself on his disciples, either by using his supra-normal powers or by argument. They must win through to the truth for themselves. Only thus, he knew, would their creed have any permanent strength or worth. So he waited; waited with a daily anxiety we may allow ourselves to picture. And at last the superb patience gained its reward. Not because it had been imposed upon them by authority, but because the conviction had grown, almost despite themselves, from within, because the teaching by word, deed, and character had made any other conclusion impossible, incredulous wonder passed into eager surmise, and then surmise was merged in certainty.

Perhaps no day brought Jesus more happiness than this. At last he felt he might venture the question on the reply to which turned all the future of his work. First, " Whom do men say that I am ? " he enquired of the twelve, and was told some of the beliefs that were current. Then came the tremendous, the decisive moment. " But whom say ye that I am ? "

And Simon Peter, spokesman for the twelve, made answer :

" Thou art the Christ; the Son of the living God ! "

CHAPTER VI

THE CRISIS

I

ALTHOUGH the Gospels are not complete
biographies, they are full enough to show
that the ministry of Jesus was divided into
well-marked periods, and that there were
great turning-points in his life on earth.
Perhaps the first was reached on that day
of his boyhood when he lingered in the
Temple, and resolved, we may believe, that
when he grew up he would be a teacher
of the Law. Another certainly was the
day of his baptism, giving a clear consciousness of his Messiahship. Critical also was
that solitary struggle which mastered temptations to misapply his powers. After the
training in Jerusalem was finished, a new
chapter opened when he returned to his

159

province of Galilee and began in Capernaum his public work as a rabbi. Then the appointment of the twelve was another definite turning-point. It signified a change of method, the results of which have endured through the centuries. Afterwards events began to shape themselves towards the final crisis. This would be reached when Jesus could feel that his hour was come, and, in a way none could disregard, publicly proclaimed himself the promised Messiah.

We shall find that the Gospels gain in fascination and coherence when we notice these main divisions into which the work of Jesus naturally falls, and observe how each stage logically prepares for the next. It is true that in regard to details the Gospels sometimes depart from strict chronological order, bringing together words or deeds that occurred at different periods because they happen to illustrate one special point in the teaching. St. Mark's, however, the earliest of the records, seems mostly to keep to the strict order of time. And whatever questions there may be whether a particular incident belongs to this or that part of the ministry, the main divisions of the work are beyond reasonable doubt. When we realize them, the pages of the Evangelists grow luminous in a new way. We understand that these writings are not—as perhaps we once supposed— mere " memorabilia," a more or less casual collection of the things which Jesus did and said, but that they set before us a story definitely connected from beginning to end, a story in which each part springs inexorably from what has gone before.

II

For the sake of clearness, let us retrace again the steps that led up to the final crisis.

The aim of Jesus the Messiah—of this Hebrew word " Christ " is, of course, the Greek equivalent—was to establish the

L

kingdom of God among men. To accomplish that was to do his Heavenly Father's will. The kingdom was to be other than popular opinion expected. It was to be spiritual, not political. It was to be set up by suasion, not force. It would gradually spread its influence, like leaven; it would gradually increase in size, like a grain of mustard-seed. It would change men's hearts, give them a new set of values, and unite them to one another and to God through love. But before it could begin, there must be teaching. The true meaning of the kingdom and the Law must be set forth. And the teaching should enable those who heard aright to discern that the teacher was himself the Messiah. That conviction, with the rest of the truth, must be encouraged to grow from within. If Jesus began by proclaiming himself the Messiah, he would be either derided or misunderstood. Either he would be attacked as another in the series of pretenders, or he would be hailed as the leader of a revolution. To guard against these risks, therefore, they who in early days did discern that Jesus was the Messiah must be charged to keep their knowledge secret. As a necessary preparation, the people must be taught the real nature of the kingdom and the Law, both of which they had been led to misinterpret. They must be brought into touch with God.

So as a rabbi, as a religious teacher and not as a politician, as one whose business was to interpret the Law and not to overthrow it, Jesus began his work in Capernaum. As we have noted, it was immediately and strikingly successful. From Capernaum Jesus, accompanied by four or five disciples, journeyed to other towns and villages within easy distance. At this stage, most of the teaching was given in the synagogues, where Jesus was welcomed by the authorities as a rabbi whose fame had already become great. At Nazareth there was local jealousy, but nowhere as yet was there official opposition. On the contrary, the right of Jesus to teach as a rabbi was unquestioned. His personality, his charm, the moving force of his words, so new in their message and so powerful in their appeal to conscience, ensured him an eager hearing. At this stage he may well have hoped to win over the national church to his views, and to convince its leaders that his revelations of God, of the Law, and of the kingdom were true. Then the national church itself would aid in spreading his message. As it did that, it would awaken also to the truth about himself. Thus, at the last, amid the welcomes of a purified and spiritualized Israel, he would enter Jerusalem, the acclaimed and recognized Messiah. There in the Temple the spiritual kingdom would have its visible centre, whence its influence would radiate through the world. The mere temporal authority of Rome would seem unimportant. And there, perhaps, the final disclosure would be made, the

divine Messiah would be transfigured and
pass in glory out of human sight. . . .

But, if ever there were such hopes, before
long they proved vain. Soon it became
evident that most of the religious leaders
would not be won over by the teaching of
Jesus, no matter how the crowds welcomed
it. Official opposition began to show itself,
and became increasingly strong. In part
it may have been due to jealousy. In
part it was stirred by the novel doctrines
about the Law which Jesus upheld. The
first quarrels were over his doctrine and
practice in regard to the sabbath. Afterwards other points of controversy de-
veloped. One traditional rule after another
—about fasting, about ceremonial washing,
about the eating of common food, about
incurring defilement in various ways—was
set aside by Jesus. The teaching he gave
about their unimportance seemed heresy.
Soon the breach between him and the
national church became complete. He

might attract and gain the admiring friendship of a Pharisee here and there. But henceforth the official policy of the religious leaders was to asperse his character, to silence him if possible, and to look for an opportunity of procuring his imprisonment and death. They were thwarted by his immense popularity with the multitudes, and their conspiracy with the Herodians to have him arrested on a political charge came to nothing. What they could do, however, was to exclude him from the synagogues. In consequence, Jesus could no longer teach as an accepted rabbi. Sometimes he was described as " the prophet from Galilee "; his seemed now more akin to the irregular and unofficial ministry of the older prophets. Yet he was still addressed as " rabbi," and still adapted to his own purpose some of their methods of instruction. So, as he had said, the work of the two great religious forces, " the Law " and " the Prophets," was conjoined in him, and he " fulfilled " them both.

Suggestion— the written gospel.
The three witnesses to future times.

THE CRISIS 167

As we have seen, his complete estrangement from the religious leaders of his age, and the personal danger in which he was placed both by their hatred and by the political suspicion of Herod, compelled him to adopt new methods. In order to secure the perpetuation of his message, he appointed the twelve apostles, gave less teaching in public, and concentrated upon training them. May we suppose that he had in mind the time when the records of his ministry would pass from the spoken to the written form, and that he trained three of the twelve with a special view to this? It seems at least to explain the difference made between Peter, James, and John and the rest. These three only, and no one else, were allowed by him to be present when he raised the daughter of Jairus. These three alone were allowed to witness the Transfiguration. These three alone were with him in Gethsemane. True, James and John were brothers. But Peter's brother, Andrew, was not allowed

Peter, James and John { Raising Jairus' daughter. Transfiguration. Gethsemane to be with Jesus and the three at these special times. Perhaps, then, the three were chosen in order that what they had seen might be included in the written Gospels. One of the oldest and most trustworthy Christian traditions affirms that St. Mark derived the material for his Gospel from Peter. By whatever hand the Fourth Gospel was edited, we may still believe that it enshrines the personal memories of John. James was beheaded by Agrippa within fourteen years of the crucifixion. Yet a recent writer attributes to him much of the information incorporated in the Gospels; arguing, for example, that St. Luke's Gospel contains "large blocks of matter drawn from the tradition of James."[1]

Of course this cannot be put forward as more than a surmise. What is clear, however, is that Jesus admitted these three apostles to a specially intimate companionship, while also he trained all the twelve

[1] *The Three Traditions in the Gospels*, by W. Lockton. (Longmans, 1927.)

Suggestion - Centurion's Servant - Mission of
Twelve - The Five Thousand.

THE CRISIS   169

so that they might understand and preach
to others the fulness of his message. For
a time he seems to have remained in
Galilee with them, chiefly in its southern
parts. But one day, when they had gone
north again to their headquarters at Capernaum, an incident occurred which may
have suggested to Jesus the possibility of
extending his work in a new way.

The detachment of troops stationed at
Capernaum was commanded by a centurion
of fine character. Though himself a Gentile and a pagan, he had defrayed the cost
of building the Jewish synagogue in the
town. And when a slave of his had fallen
ill, this centurion showed practical sympathy of a kind rare enough in that age
among slave-owners. Hearing that the
great healer was in the town, he begged
for the assistance of Jesus, who said that
he would come and heal the slave. But
the centurion demurred. This was needless, he said. The famous rabbi would
incur technical defilement by entering the

house of a Gentile. As a soldier, he knew that commands were obeyed without the personal presence of the authority who issued them. Jesus, he was sure, had authority over invisible powers. Let him but give them his command, and the slave would be healed. As both St. Matthew's and St. Luke's Gospels frankly state, Jesus was astonished by this serene and confident faith. He " marvelled " at it. It was the more striking because he who showed it was a Gentile. Not in Israel, said Jesus, had he found such faith as this. It may have encouraged him to go, as he did not long afterwards, into the pagan country north of Galilee. He could do much for its inhabitants if they were capable of faith such as this centurion had shown.

But before leaving his own province of Galilee, he would try to send his message to places in it which he himself had been unable to visit. There was much ground still to be covered. So he sent out no fewer than six missions, to work at the same time in different directions. Two by two the twelve went forth. They were to preach repentance, and they were given special power to cast out evil spirits and to heal by anointing with oil—not a method which Jesus himself ever used. They were to take but the least possible equipment, so that they might not be mistaken for persons travelling on business or for pleasure. They would be maintained by the people they visited, but they were not to thrust themselves upon unwilling hosts or hearers; these, with a solemn warning, they were to leave behind. And for the present they were to limit their work strictly to the Jews. So they went their various ways; we may imagine with what farewells and encouragement from their master.

During their mission in Galilee, Jesus seems to have visited Jerusalem. Then he returned, to meet the twelve at the time and place he had appointed. But now Galilee had become even more dangerous

for him than it had been before. The
knowledge that six separate missions were
wandering through his land and proclaiming
the advent of some strange kingdom increased the suspicions of Herod Antipas
about Jesus and his followers. Evidently,
too, the mission of the twelve would be
regarded as a direct challenge by the
religious authorities. Much as the Pharisees
had resented the doctrine of Jesus, as yet
they had not doubted his credentials as a
rabbi. But that he should despatch twelve
fishermen and peasants—with an ex-publican among them!—to spread his heresies
up and down the country seemed intoler-
able. Thus Galilee was no longer a province in which Jesus could stay with safety
for any length of time.

The place, however, where Jesus had
commanded the twelve to rejoin him was
in Galilee. Probably it was Capernaum;
certainly it was on the Lake. At once the
eager apostles began to pour out their
reports of " all things, whatsoever they

had done, and whatsoever they had taught."
But the little group was quickly surrounded
by a restless, shifting crowd, insistent with
questions, with clamorous welcome, with
demands for miracles. The scene is painted
vividly by the evangelists. Jesus wished
to be alone with the twelve. In that
setting, quiet talk with them was impossible. " ' Come ye yourselves apart into
a desert place and rest awhile,' " he said.
" For there were many coming and going,
and they had no leisure so much as to
eat." So in " the boat "—the boat always
kept ready for their use in case of sudden
need for flight—they crossed to the other
side. But the crowd saw them put off,
and ran on foot round the northern end of
the Lake, and arrived first on the opposite
coast. When Jesus and the apostles
beached their boat, instead of the quiet
seclusion on which they had counted, they
found the very crowd they had thought to
have left behind at Capernaum waiting to
meet them !

We get a glimpse of the superb equanimity, the undefeated kindness of Jesus, when we note that, so far from being exasperated by the untimely demands of these people, he " had compassion on them, and began to teach them many things." He had spent the morning in trying to hear the reports of the twelve, while having to deal with the continual interruptions and requests of the crowd. There was no leisure for the midday meal. He made the voyage across the Lake, only to find the multitude awaiting him. Hour after hour he endured the further strain of teaching some five thousand people in the open air. When at last " the day was now far spent," he made them sit in orderly fashion on the grass, and used his supernatural powers to give them food. But the effect of this deed was disastrous. It so stirred the enthusiasm of the people that they tried to seize Jesus in order to make him their king. In haste, lest they too should be infected by the idea, Jesus compelled the

twelve to embark again and to cross the
seven miles of water, " while he himself
sendeth the multitude away." At last he
managed to quiet and dismiss them. " And
when he had taken leave of them," not
even then, as we might suppose, did he
rest ! No; " he departed into the mountain to pray." At all costs he must have
solitary communion with his Father. Yet
this again was interrupted. From the
height where he prayed he saw—for it was
the time of the paschal full moon—his
disciples " distressed in rowing, for the
wind was contrary." So he comes to
them wonderfully across the water and
calms the storm. By this time it is " the
fourth watch of the night "—3 a.m. When
at last they landed again on the western
side of the Lake, " straightway the people
knew him," and hurried to fetch their sick
folk that they might be healed.

Such were twenty-four hours in the
working life of Jesus.

III

But it was clear that the Galilæan ministry was finished. Jesus must hasten to escape out of the territory of Herod Antipas. What had just happened, the assemblage of many thousands and their misguided attempt to make Jesus their king, would impel the Government to take action, and would give them the pretext they needed. Moreover, the animosity of the ecclesiastical authorities in Galilee was stirred afresh by a deputation of Pharisees and Sadducees from Jerusalem. This was presumably a result of the visit recently paid by Jesus to the capital. Its significance only becomes clear when we recollect that Pharisees and Sadducees were rival sects, violently opposed to one another. That they should now unite in order to attack Jesus was a measure of their hatred against him. Their presence and efforts to entrap him were another reason for quitting Galilee. Finally, Jesus desired, as we have seen, leisure and quiet in order that he might concentrate on his task of instructing the twelve. He could not carry out this purpose among the clamorous throng, or where at any moment he might be arrested by Herod's officers. So he and the twelve were compelled to fly from Galilee. Afterwards they only entered it at intervals for a few days at a time when conditions were favourable, then again retreating across the border before their presence was generally known.

First they went to the far north-west, staying in the coast district near Tyre and Sidon. Here his knowledge of Greek would be of service to Jesus. It enabled him to talk with a Greek-speaking Phœnician woman, whose nimble wit won for her the healing of her daughter. When he travels south again, he carefully keeps outside the territory of Antipas. For a time he was in Philip's land, in and near Cæsarea Philippi, and then in that strange Hellenic colony of ten cities known as Decapolis. During

M

these months he was willing to use his powers as a healer when eager supplicants asked his help, but he attempted no public teaching by word. He gave his strength to training the twelve. He was preparing himself also for the crisis, and spent much time in solitary prayer. It is curious to notice how powerfully the symbolism of the hills appealed to him. When he had climbed them, he seemed to feel that he had gained a loftier level in more than a physical sense. The remoteness, the silences, the winds and wide views of a hill aided his communion with his Father. Whenever he could, he withdrew from the plains to the heights.

The Transfiguration

One evening, in these months of travel with the twelve, Jesus came to Hermon; that great mountain in the north country, near the source of the Jordan, snow-crowned through most of the year, and rising to a height of more than nine thousand feet. Jesus ascended one of its outlying spurs. He took with him Peter, James, and John, those three witnesses to future times. The darkness fell, and while Jesus still prayed, his disciples slept. Then they were roused by a sudden brightness, and with dazzled eyes saw their master standing radiant and transfigured. He was speaking to two strangers, and their converse showed that these were Moses and Elijah. They had revisited the earth to stand, the traditional founders of the Law and the Prophets, beside him who had come to end the ancient animosity between the two forms of religion, and to fulfil them both. Jesus told them of what must befall him in Jerusalem. And Peter, half awake and wholly terrified, stammered incoherent words. A cloud overshadowed them, and there was a Voice which said: "This is My beloved son; hear ye him." When the cloud dispersed, Prophet and Lawgiver had vanished: Jesus remained. He forbade the three to tell any, even the other

apostles, what they had seen, until the
time should come when he had died and
conquered death. . . .

An amazing story. What are we to
make of it? The more we study the simplicity, directness, restraint, and candour
with which it is told by each of the first
three Gospels, the more assured we may
feel that these are records of a genuine
experience. To rationalize it as a phantasy
or to dismiss it as a fabrication seem alike
impossible. Even the frankness with which
Peter's bemused babble (" for he knew not
what he said ") is given confirms its truthfulness. An imagined scene of this kind
would have been described very differently.
It is the story of a great spiritual experience, and of a real spiritual experience.
That we can affirm with confidence, and
more than that we need not wish to say.
The precise mode of its happening must
remain beyond our understanding. Psycho-
logical explanations of its source are as

unsatisfying as allegorical interpretations of its meaning. There are moments, and this is one, when we shall be wise if we accept the limitations of human knowledge, and are content to revere.

IV

Yet it is not rash to believe that, as the baptism brought Jesus inspiration for the beginning of his ministry, so the transfiguration gave him added strength as he neared its crisis and its close. And of this, surely, he had need, for how much there was to discourage at this time ! Probably between two and three years had passed since he began his work in Galilee. We have noted how its first bright promise of growing success had passed away. And it was of sinister omen that the change had been brought about by outside influence. Even the Pharisees in Galilee had not been openly hostile until

they were made so by emissaries from
Jerusalem. It was true that Jesus had not
lost his hold upon the Galilæan people.
Many, no doubt, especially among the upper
classes, had been turned against him by
the example of their religious leaders.
Others were chagrined by his failure to
initiate a political revolution. Yet there
were hundreds to whom his touch had
brought healing, and more to whom his
words had given faith and strength and
happiness. As for the great mass of the
people, it was true that they misunderstood much of the teaching, and, in particular, failed utterly to understand the
nature of the kingdom which Jesus had
laboured to set before them clearly. It
was true, as he complained, that they sought
him often from unworthy motives, as when
they came " because they ate of the loaves
and were filled." Yet they sought him,
with feelings in which curiosity and awe
and love all had their part. To the last,

faithful and loyal Galileans

whenever he was known to be in Galilee, they rushed in thousands to welcome him. The efforts of their official religious teachers to keep them away were vain.

Here, then, was abundance of material for further ministry. If as yet but few of these affectionate people had managed to grasp his real message, they might be taught it in time. If, having trained his apostles and fitted them to co-operate with him, Jesus could hold further missions in Galilee, plainly they would be fruitful of result. But this was just what he could not do. An unholy alliance between the emissaries from Jerusalem and Herod had outlawed him, in effect, from his own province. Now he could but enter its borders for the briefest of secret visits. To recommence preaching there would mean his prompt arrest. We may dare to imagine the bitterness of this disappointment, of finding himself excluded from his own country and its eager people, of having no further chance to win them over to his doctrine of the kingdom.

Where, then, should he turn? He was safe, and welcomed, in the pagan north. He was safe in Perea, or elsewhere on the east side of the Jordan. But not in these districts was his work to be done. What of Judæa, and Jerusalem itself? It was in Jerusalem, according to those ancient prophecies which the Jews studied, that the Messiah would declare himself. He would enter the city as king; he would come suddenly to the Temple. Therefore the first effort of every false Christ that had arisen had been to obtain possession of the Temple. But his visits to Jerusalem had shown Jesus all too plainly the temper of its people. He had found no success there, such as had brightened the early months in Galilee. The predominant influence was that of the Sadducees, whose hatred was more malignant than that of the Pharisees and their scribes in Galilee. The Pharisees had a religion, perverted and sterile though it was. The Sadducees were worldly and of sordid mind; not among the Sadducees could Jesus find a Nicodemus. Yet in Jerusalem the Pharisees were willing to combine with their hated rivals in order to destroy Jesus. At a much earlier stage of the ministry, the Fourth Gospel affirms that " Jesus walked in Galilee; for he would not walk in Judæa, because the Jews "—a name this Gospel limits to the inhabitants of Judæa—" sought to kill him." And in Jerusalem, though some of the multitudes said " he is a good man," " no man spake of him openly, for fear of the Jews."

What was he to do? Galilee was closed to him. For months he had spent his strength in training the twelve, and, dense and unreceptive as they had often seemed, there was not much more which, at this stage, he could do for them. How was the kingdom of God to be set up? As we have seen, it was to be a society of mankind linked with God and one another by love; its law the law of service, its charter the Father's benediction. All within it must be docile as little children are, ready to accept its new standard of values, brave to fight evil in themselves and in the world, eager at all costs to tune their wills with the will of God. Such as these would form the Kingdom; such as these would have passed from death into life.

Jesus had planned to work for some years as a rabbi, the better to expound the nature and laws of this spiritual kingdom. He would show how Law and prophets had prepared for it, when their doctrines were rightly understood. He would work by means of the national church, which in turn would spread his Gospel. From district to district it would spread. From belief in this kingdom would grow belief in himself as the promised king. Then this spiritual kingdom would be formally

inaugurated in Jerusalem, and his own
divine Messiahship would supersede the
lower and mistaken hopes of a political
upheaval. From Jerusalem the good news
would go forth into all the world, and all
the world would be transformed and transfigured into a part of the kingdom of God.

That plan had failed. Was there any
other method by which the kingdom could
be established? There was one. There
was only one. More and more clearly
Jesus saw this other way to be inevitable
if he was to fulfil his divine mission and
accomplish his Father's will. He would
make a public entry into Jerusalem, as
the Messiah was expected to do, at the
coming Passover. He would assert himself
as the Christ. He would exercise his
authority in the Temple. And the swift
result, beyond question, must be his suffering, and torture, and death. But physical
death could not touch his imperishable life.
After a short space, sufficient to show that

his death, as men count death, was no
illusion, his life would again be manifested
to those who loved him. And when he
was no longer visibly among them, its
power would be perpetuated by the divine
spirit. Thus his death would succeed where
his life had failed. He would die, he would
be raised from the dead. So, after all, the
kingdom would be inaugurated in Jerusalem. So by degrees it would spread
throughout the world. So would Jesus the
crucified be revealed as Jesus the Christ.

V

He tried to prepare the twelve for what
must befall him. But he tried in vain. By
a strange paradox, it was the very faith to
which they had recently won through that
now made his words to them incredible.
If in the past he had told them that he
was to be crucified, they would have been
aghast—yet they might have believed it.

But now they were sure, as Peter had said, that he was the Christ, the son of the living God. And that the promised Messiah should suffer death as a criminal was unthinkable. The idea that God could permit it seemed grotesque. How was the promised work of deliverance to be done if the Messiah perished? Their master had said much that was hard to accept, but this went beyond all bounds. They merely dismissed it as incomprehensible. They found it a relief to get back to sane conversation among themselves. Let us talk of practical things, said they. When Jesus has set up his kingdom in Jerusalem, to which of us will he give the most important posts? Again and again he tried to make them understand that he meant what he said, but vainly. He had to lack human sympathy as the great crisis came near.

Yet he began to prepare for the journey towards Jerusalem. He paid, with necessary secrecy, a final visit to Capernaum

and the house there which had been his
second home. Then he went south. As
soon as he had crossed the border into
Samaria, he resumed the methods of work
which he had laid aside during the months
of training the twelve. He began again a
public ministry. In St. Mark's words,
" multitudes come together unto him again,
and, as he was wont, he taught them again."
He recruited many new disciples, and
despatched no fewer than seventy of them,
two and two, as advance messengers to
the towns and villages which he himself
proposed to visit later. Afterwards he
worked in Perea. His own immense burden, his prevision of the final choice he
must make, never lessened his readiness to
heal the sick, to comfort the sorrowful, to
help all that came with their multitudinous
and often obtuse questions.

Twice in this period he seems, while
leaving his disciples elsewhere, to have
visited Jerusalem, and to have taught

there. But he found nothing to lift the shadow, nothing to change his tragic certainty of what would befall him when he entered the city as the Messiah. A chance word spoken during one of these visits possibly reveals how deeply the strain of these last few months had set its mark upon Jesus. Challenging a mystic utterance of his, a bystander observed : " Thou art not yet fifty years old." The speaker, who judged from his personal appearance, perhaps guessed him to be forty-five or thereabouts. In fact, Jesus was in his thirty-third year ! Yet can we wonder if his face had aged prematurely since the day when he began to see the cross at the end of his road ?

VI

Then the crisis came. The final decision had to be made. It was the supreme hour. He must be alone. He had sent the twelve to meet their Galilæan friends and relatives who even now were streaming from the north towards Jerusalem, where they must keep the Passover. The Galilæans mostly travelled by the eastern road, to avoid passing through Samaria, " for the Jews have no dealings with the Samaritans." Jesus himself seems to have been some-where near Jericho at this time, about twenty miles from Jerusalem. The great highway was near him. In which direction should he walk along it? It was not too late to alter his decision. He could go to the north. It led to security. It led to places where he would be welcome. It led to towns and villages where he could con-tinue to teach and heal. Or he could go south. It led to—the cross. We say that word easily now, and even its symbolism is often forgotten. It was different in days when the mere word caused the strongest to shudder, when it stood for every circum-stance of torture and humiliation, pre-

luding hours of unimaginable agony. . . .
There was, humanly speaking, no need to
take it. Jesus was free. He was under no
compulsion, except that of love and the
conviction, which would not yield, that
thus only could the Father's purpose be
accomplished and the kingdom of God set
up. North and south lay the road. We
know nothing of that hour of decision,
when the whole future history of man was
in the balance. The Gospels are silent
concerning it.

But the earliest of them gives us a picture
of Jesus as he emerged from that supreme
crisis and conflict of the soul. It gives us
the picture in simple words which become
unforgettable when their significance is
realized. The twelve with other pilgrims
are coming along the road towards Jerusalem. Suddenly Jesus steps forward from
some spot where he has been awaiting them,
and places himself at their head. The
choice is made. He is walking south—to

N

the cross. But what was this look on his face, what was this new mysterious sense of awe that they felt? Here is the simple record :

" And they were in the way, going up to Jerusalem; and Jesus was going before them; and they were amazed; and they that followed were afraid."

They could not account for their sudden fear. They did not know what new power in him it was that stirred this amazement. The twelve dared not ask, or walk beside him pouring out their eager words, as was their wont. They were amazed. Alone, with that awe-compelling look upon his face, he went before them. But presently, " he took again the twelve, and began to tell them the things that were to happen unto him."

Let the picture stand. To mar it by comments would be inexcusable.

Yet among the Galilæan pilgrims who

followed the apostles a question woke and persisted. It persists still. Was Jesus no more than an amiable ex-carpenter of Nazareth? " The difficulties of belief " is a common phrase. But is there anything in the world so difficult, so impossible, to believe as this?

CHAPTER VII

THE LAST DAYS

I

IN describing the three years' ministry of Jesus, St. Mark's Gospel gives no less than a third of its space to the last seven days. No doubt Peter's recollections of that tremendous period would be specially full and vivid, and from Peter's recollections most of the material for this Gospel was derived. Yet even this would hardly account for the great detail with which the events of the last week are set forth. There may be a simple explanation. We have the account of the arrest in the olive-orchard named Gethsemane. We are told how all the disciples fled. We are told how the guard led away Jesus to the high priest.

But between these sentences suddenly this is interpolated :

" And a certain young man "—a young man, that means, whose name the writer could give if he chose—" followed with him, having a linen cloth cast about him, over his naked body : and they lay hold on him ; but he left the linen cloth and fled naked."

Why is the main narrative suddenly broken off in order that we may be told of this incident ? By itself, it appears quite pointless. Various attempts have been made to account for its insertion, and one of them seems wholly satisfying. This " certain young man " was the writer of the Gospel himself. Perhaps his house adjoined the orchard.[1] Before dawn he

---

[1] Of which, again, he may have been the owner. It is to be noted that the word translated " linen cloth " means rich and costly linen, such as none but a wealthy man would have had. On the other hand, Mark's mother owned a house *within* the city some fourteen years later (Acts xii. 12).

was roused by the sound of voices and the
flare of torches. He rose, hastily threw a
wrap round him, and dashed out. As he
pushed his way towards Jesus, the guards,
fearing an attempt at rescue, tried to seize
him. His wrap remained in their hands as
he turned and fled. A happening trivial in
itself, but how much it would mean to Mark
in later days, when he had learnt to worship
Jesus! Although he would not mention
himself by name, he could not resist includ-
ing his own little part in the story of that
night. If, too, Mark was in Jerusalem
through this week, and was himself a
witness of much that happened there, we
can understand why he devotes a third or
more of his whole work to describing these
days. Here he can use, not only Peter's
reminiscences, but his own. And therefore
these chapters of his have a special historical value. His long account is supplemented by some details obtained by the
other evangelists from other sources. In

fact, we know far more of the last week than of any other period in the life of Jesus.

The sabbath—that is, the Saturday before what we keep now as Palm Sunday—he spent at Bethany, about two miles from Jerusalem, in the house of friends he loved —Lazarus, Martha, and Mary. When the sabbath ended, at 6 p.m., he finished his preparations for the morrow. And then, on the first day of the week, he made his solemn entry into the city as the Christ, the Messiah promised to Israel. Every religious Jew had studied the prophecies about the Messiah. There was a passage in Zechariah predicting the manner of his entry into Jerusalem : " Rejoice greatly, O daughter of Zion; shout, O daughter of Jerusalem : behold, thy king cometh unto thee : he is just, and having salvation; lowly, and riding upon an ass, even upon a colt the foal of an ass." Therefore when Jesus placed himself among the Galilæans and other strangers who were pouring towards Jerusalem, and rode in their midst seated upon an ass, this was no act of humility. It was a regal challenge. It was a definite assertion, which none could misunderstand, that he claimed to be the Messiah, the Lord God's Christ, the king of Israel.

The Galilæans joyfully recognized that sign, and did him homage. They strewed the road with palms, they carpeted it with their cloaks. " And they that went before, and they that followed, cried : Hosanna ! Blessed is he that cometh in the name of the Lord ! Blessed is the kingdom that cometh ! Hosanna in the highest ! " As the procession entered the city, the Pharisees also recognized the sign, and scowled. " Rabbi," they said—so to address him was to deny that higher title which the pæans of the crowd conceded—" Rabbi, rebuke thy disciples." With a solemn pride and joy, that for a moment shone through humility and sorrow, Jesus an-

swered : " I tell you that if these should
hold their peace, the stones would immediately cry out." And, adds the Matthæan
Gospel, when he was come into Jerusalem,
all the city was stirred as by an earthquake
—such is the literal meaning of the word.
" Who is this? " asked the people of
Jerusalem. Then, again in accordance with
Messianic prophecies, and thus confirming
the belief of his followers, Jesus made his
way towards the Temple.

II

And here we may guard ourselves against
a misinterpretation of the facts that followed—a misinterpretation curiously common and persistent. It has been pop-
ularized by countless sermons. It runs
somewhat as follows :—As Jesus rode into
Jerusalem, fulfilling the signs of the prophet,
the people were sure that he was the
Messiah. As such they acclaimed him.

Then, when he reached the Temple, they
waited confidently for his call to action.
He would summon them to rise in God's
name, and, aided by His power, to overthrow the rule of Rome. But he said no
word of that kind. Their enthusiasm vanished. They were disappointed and dismayed. They felt that they had been
duped. Their ardour for Jesus changed
into anger against him. His enemies made
adroit use of this reaction. The priests
and scribes easily induced the people to
demand that he should be put to death.
The same voices that had cried " Hosanna "
on Palm Sunday shouted " Crucify ! " on
Good Friday. And this has become among
preachers almost a stock illustration of
human fickleness.

Yet, when we examine the Gospels with
care, we find that this account is quite at
variance with their narratives. In point
of fact, while the Jews certainly expected
the Messiah to lead them to national

independence, they would not anticipate a
rising to be begun during the week of the
Passover. They would look for a call to
arms to be given only when this, the most
solemn of their religious festivals, was
ended. That is, however, a detail. The
main point to be noticed is that the people
who did homage to Jesus as the Messiah
were quite other than those who clamoured
for his death. The former was a Galilæan
crowd, composed of pilgrims coming from
the north to keep the Passover. The procession began at Bethany, two miles away,
and thence escorted Jesus in triumph into
the city. The inhabitants of Jerusalem
had no part in the demonstration. They
were startled by it, and demanded, " Who is
this ? " To which the answer was : " This
is the prophet, Jesus, from Nazareth in
Galilee." We may notice two points in
that reply : first, that these Galilæans
took pride in saying that it was from their
province that Jesus came. And, secondly,

that, chilled by the scorn of the Jerusalem folk for the provincials, they dared not say "this is the Messiah," though this they believed him to be. They ventured only to describe him as "the prophet."

The other, that which shouted "Crucify!" was a Jerusalem crowd. Probably not a very large one; it would not need a great crowd to throng the forecourt of the Prætorium. The people composing it were dwellers in Jerusalem, accustomed to do the bidding of the powerful Temple rulers. Probably not a few of them were those parasites of whom Jesus had cleansed the Temple a few days earlier. Easily enough would they be persuaded to ask for the release of Barabbas rather than of Jesus.

To suppose that the same people shouted "Hosanna!" and "Crucify!" is grossly to slander those loyal Galilæans. They formed a vast multitude, coming as they did from a whole province. They far outnumbered the usual residents in Jerusalem.

Instead of being fickle and hastening the death of Jesus, they were a barrier between him and his enemies, through which only an apostle's treachery broke at the last. So far from conniving at his death, day after day their unchanged fidelity kept him alive. St. Luke is at special pains to make this clear. Let us turn to his statements. On the Monday, the enemies of Jesus "could not find what they might do, for all the people hung upon him, listening." On the Tuesday, "the scribes and priests sought to lay hands on him in that very hour, and they feared the people." Again on the Wednesday, "the chief priests and scribes sought how they might put him to death, for they feared the people." [1] But before Wednesday was over, Iscariot had made his shameful pact. That ended all. In the following night the priests effected their purpose, while those thousands of Galilæans, and those many others whom the

[1] St. Luke xix. 47, 48; xx. 19; xxii. 2.

words of Jesus had won over since the
Sunday, were asleep. Yet the Galilæan
loyalty had not been vain. It had pro-
longed till Friday the life of Jesus, which
else had been cut short on Palm Sunday.
How much those few days were to mean
then and afterwards to the disciples; how
rich they were in wonderful deeds and
words preserved for every age ! Had it not
been for the Galilæans, the Gospels must
have lacked those pages. We wrong their
memory when we misread and pervert clear
evidence in order to point a moral, and
affirm, which certainly is false, that the lips
which said " Hosanna " were those which
said " Crucify."

Popular talk, again, is apt to wrong the
Jewish nation as a whole, by attributing the
murder of Jesus to national rejection and
hatred of him. The evidence of the Gospel
narratives shows that his actual enemies
were very powerful but very few. As for
the general mass of people, their feelings

towards him were of every kind—passionate devotion and belief, hesitating wonder, indifference, scepticism, derision. But who were his active opponents? In Galilee, Herod and the officials of his government; also, after a while, the Pharisees and Pharisaic scribes, though their hostility did not become pronounced until it was stirred up by emissaries in Jerusalem. It was here that fierce opposition to Jesus had its centre. The enmity of Herod was mixed with, if not allayed by, sheer curiosity to see the man of whom such strange stories were current. But the religious authorities at Jerusalem longed simply for his destruction. Their reasons are clear. To begin with, we should remember—and the fact has its bearing upon what has been said in the preceding paragraph—that the Jerusalem authorities had the greatest contempt for all Galilæans, as uncouth and uncultured provincials. Then we have seen how completely the teaching by word and deed of

Jesus had refuted the legalism, with its grotesque idea of " righteousness," upheld by the Pharisees and their scribes. With them, for the sole purpose of destroying Jesus, their bitter rivals the Sadducees combined. They were a small, wealthy, aristocratic, and most powerful party. To it most of the priests belonged, and it was the prevailing force on the Sanhedrin, the great religious council of the nation. In short, it was not the Jewish people as a whole, or even the inhabitants of Jerusalem, that put Jesus to death. This was wholly the deed of the religious authorities, with the help of a Roman official as their most reluctant tool.

III

As the triumphant entry on Palm Sunday had directly challenged and exasperated the Pharisees, so on the next day Jesus provoked the fierce anger of the Sadducees.

It was a popular expectation, based partly on words of the prophets, that the Messiah would occupy the Temple, and use it as the stronghold from which to direct a campaign against Rome. But this Messiah entered the Temple, not to fortify it as a stronghold, but to purify it as a House of Prayer. The desecration he saw moved him to anger. At this time the " court of the Gentiles " was used as a money-exchange, a market, and a public thorough-fare. Every Jew had to pay a yearly tribute of a half-shekel to the Temple authorities, and the annual total received in this way has been computed at £76,000. The payment had to be made in the special Hebrew coinage. Roman, Persian, Syrian, Egyptian, and Greek money were all in circulation among the Jews. Therefore a few weeks before each Passover the money-changers' tables were set up in the Temple, and their lucrative business began. Even at the statutory rate of commission, their

o

annual profits have been reckoned at about £9,000. But inevitably they combined usury with their legitimate business. It is easy to picture the scene witnessed under the Temple roof in the days immediately before the Passover, when these Oriental bankers were at the height of their trade— the clink of money-bags, the doubtful weighing of heaps of coins, the clamorous din of bargaining, argument, expostulation over the rate of exchange. Beside this money-changing, and in the same court of the Temple—a court dedicated to prayer ! —a live-stock market was in progress. Here farmers chaffered over the price of animals they wished to sell to the Temple dealers. Here customers bought, with the shrill haggling of an Eastern bazaar, the doves they required for ritual offerings. Between the stalls of dealers and money-changers, and through the mob of purchasers, struggled family parties, laden with earthen vessels and other impedimenta.

For a custom had grown of using this part of the Temple as a short cut from the city to the Mount of Olives, where many encamped through the crowded week of Passover.

Upon that scene of tumultuous irreverence suddenly came Jesus. Let what followed be told in the words of an eyewitness :

" He cast out them that sold and them that bought in the Temple, and overthrew the tables of the money-changers, and the seats of them that sold the doves, and he would not suffer that any man should carry a vessel through the Temple."

The restraint of this concise sentence must not blind us to the dramatic intensity and marvel of the event it describes. Here is an episode not to be forgotten when we try to realize the Jesus of the Gospels. As we watch his disciplined fury, we amend that false idea of him as always " meek and gentle." We think of the physical strength shown as the merchants' stalls were over-turned, as the money-changers' tables crashed jingling on the pavement. We think of the moral strength—do not the facts compel us to say the superhuman power?—with which, single-handed, he routed an indignant multitude, driving them shrinking and terrified before him.

It was not this rabble only that his wrath touched. The chief priests knew themselves to be defied and discredited, for it was they who had sanctioned, for their own gain, this misuse of the House of Prayer. We cannot wonder that when " they heard it, they sought to destroy him."

IV

Jesus had spent the Sunday night, like the Saturday, at Bethany, returning to the city on the following morning. But to do that again in the evening meant a two-mile walk along a crowded road, where almost at every step he would be checked and questioned by the curious; where, too, he might be ambushed by his enemies, made doubly fierce by his deeds on Sunday and Monday—the Messianic procession, the cleansing of the Temple. The fatigue of that walk, with all its risk and strain, after a day of tremendous work was clearly undesirable. Moreover, he wished to be with his disciples, who probably were afraid both for themselves and him. In his earlier visits to Jerusalem he had made some friends, who were indeed disciples— but, like Nicodemus, " secretly, for fear of the Jews." With them he had made arrangements in advance. From one he would borrow the ass upon which he was to ride. Another would lend him a large upper room where he could eat the Passover meal with his disciples. To each of these at the right moment a disciple would come with a pre-arranged sentence, which the lender would recognize.

There was a third friend—reasons for
identifying him with St. Mark have already
been given—who owned a walled orchard,
"Gethsemane," [1] on the Mount of Olives.
With him Jesus arranged that he and his
disciples should have the use of this orchard
as their resting-place. Bivouacking would
entail no hardship in the warmth of late
April, and the Paschal moon was at its full.
This was far better than a daily journey to
and from Bethany. The orchard was but a
short distance outside the walls of the city.
Yet it was private property and entirely
secluded. Here Jesus could find rest after
the tremendous work of his daily public
ministry. Here he could be alone with his
apostles, and give them the further teaching he desired without fear of interruption.
And here he and they could sleep at peace.
If his enemies, as was likely enough, tried

---

[1] The name means, literally, "oil-press." The
Greek word by which St. Mark describes it means "an
enclosed plot of ground."

to catch and arrest him by night in the city
—their " fear of the people " made him safe
by day—they would not find him. None
would know where he had gone. And
none did know, until " Judas, one of the
twelve," sold the secret.

So the last three days of public ministry
began. In these last days, as in the first
at Capernaum long before, Jesus came
before the people as an accredited rabbi.
Even then, he would not force upon them
his Messianic claims. On the Sunday and
Monday his actions had made them un-
mistakably plain. It was for the people to
accept or reject them. Now he would
teach. At the time of the great religious
feasts, the rabbis sat in the shade of the
great cloisters enclosing the outer court of
the Temple, and there held instruction-
classes. The people gathered round whatever rabbi they preferred, asking questions.
and listening to his exposition of the Law.
To that work, then, Jesus now gave himself.

Early each morning he came down from the slope of the Mount of Olives, crossed the ravine at its foot, entered the Temple, took his accustomed seat in the cloisters, and there taught, hour after hour. When at evening the hour came for the Temple to be closed and the last of the listeners reluctantly to leave, he went again to Gethsemane, instructed his apostles, looked with them over the valley towards Jerusalem and wept over it, and then prayed and rested until the dawn. St. Luke gives us the picture : " Every day he was teaching in the Temple; and every night he went out, and lodged in the mount that is called the Mount of Olives. And all the people came early in the morning to him in the Temple, to hear him."

His enemies, afraid to use force, proposed to themselves another plan. If they could not at once destroy him, perhaps they could discredit him. Emissaries of theirs should join the crowd gathered about him, and, in the guise of learners, should ask carefully-prepared questions—questions which, as it seemed, he could neither dare to answer nor evade answering.

But there was no pretence of courtesy in the first question. It came from the chief priests and scribes, and was a blunt challenge of his right to teach. " You sit here," they said in effect, " as a duly-authorized rabbi. Indeed, from the first you have taught, in synagogues and elsewhere, as ' one having authority,' as an authorized teacher of the Law. But where are your credentials? By what kind "—that is the precise force of the word used — " of authority doest thou these things? and who gave thee this authority? " Jesus replied with a counter-question. What would they say of John's ministry of baptism? Was John's " authority " for undertaking it derived from the Sanhedrin or any human source? Or did a commission from God himself make human credentials needless?

"And they reasoned within themselves, saying, If we shall say, From heaven : he will say, Why did ye not believe him? But if we shall say, From men; all the people will stone us, for they be persuaded that John was a prophet. And they answered that they knew not whence it was. And Jesus said unto them, Neither tell I you by what authority I do these things."

Next came Pharisees and Herodians, with every appearance of deference. "Rabbi," they began (" observe, we are not like those unmannerly priests, questioning thy right to this title!")—"Rabbi, we know that thou art true, and teachest the way of God in truth "—and then followed the question about "giving"—such was the word they used—the tribute to Rome. The answer "Yes," they reckoned, must mean popular disfavour; he could not be thought the Messiah who acquiesced in Roman rule; the answer "No" would be treason, with the news of which they would hasten to Pilate. But the unexpected reply of Jesus discomfited them. Here was no question of " giving," but of paying what was lawfully due. " Fetch me a denarius," he said. St. Mark supplies us with the word used; St. Matthew and St. Luke, missing its point, substitute " show." It had to be brought from outside; there were no Roman coins within the Temple now that the money-changers had been expelled! And when he had bidden them observe whose were " the image and superscription " on it, he said : " Pay to Cæsar what belongs to Cæsar; pay to God what belongs to God." His questioners " could not take hold of the saying "; they were reduced to sullen silence.

Lastly, the Sadducees took their turn. It would be a triumph to discomfit Jesus. It would be a triumph to succeed where their rivals the Pharisees had failed. And it would be a special triumph if they could succeed by means of a question deriding belief in a future life—a doctrine the

Pharisees held, and Sadducees rejected.
But for the purpose they had nothing
better than an ancient conundrum to pro-
pound, the futility of which Jesus quickly
exposed. " Rabbi, thou hast well said ! "
cried a Pharisaic scribe, unable to hide his
pleasure at the rout of the Sadducees.
And from that time no man durst ask
Jesus any more dishonest questions.

Thereafter he was free to teach those who
were eager to learn. In answer to a lawyer,
he reaffirmed his supreme commandment of
love. He denounced the insincerity of
Pharisees and scribes with pitiless invective.
He instructed the people by wonderful
parables. He spoke of his own fate, and
of the doom which should befall Jerusalem ;
a theme to which he returned when he was
alone with the twelve on the Mount of
Olives. With this were mingled solemn
visions of an ultimate world-judgment,
clothed in imagery which he took over and
adapted from the apocalyptic writings.

V

So day by day Jesus the teacher continued his work, resolute to use to the utmost whatever time remained for him. His foes complained bitterly that "the whole world is gone after him." And as his influence upon the people increased, so did the jealous rage of his enemies. On the Wednesday they held an informal meeting at the high priest's house, to consider how they might effect his capture and destruction. But reluctantly they agreed that their vengeance must wait until after the Passover, when the Galilæans had returned to their own province. "Not during the feast," they said, "lest haply there shall be a tumult of the people." Their words (recorded by St. Mark) again refute any idea that the multitude's devotion to Jesus ended with Palm Sunday.

Perhaps the gathering in Caiaphas's house had just agreed with reluctance upon the policy of delay, and was about to break up, when Iscariot, having learnt of the meeting and guessed its purpose, came to make his proposal. Awful and unutterably base though it was, the priests rejoiced at this easy and unexpected means of accomplishing their purpose. Readily they promised the traitor his wages. The bargain was concluded. Who can say what led Judas to his downfall? Greed of money, the disappointed ambition of one who had counted on high office in an early kingdom, anger at the rebuke given when he complained of the " wasted " ointment—each of these may have had a part, or there may have been quite other causes, of which we know nothing. Attempts have been made to minimize the guilt of Judas. It has been supposed, for instance, that he wished merely to force Jesus into showing his divine power. By means of it he must repel any attack by the priests' officers, and thus all would be convinced beyond doubt

that he was the Messiah. But, however
ingenious they may seem, attempts to
exculpate Judas fail when we recall the
words spoken of him by his master. Jesus
showed himself wonderfully kind and lenient
to his disciples. He forgave their coward-
ice, their broken promises, their desertion
of him in the hour of danger. When
therefore he says :

" The Son of man goeth, even as it is
written of him, but woe unto that man
through whom the Son of man is betrayed !
Good were it for that man if he had not
been born "—

we are sure that it was not of a merely
ill-judged but well-meant deed that these
awful words were spoken.

Having slunk away from the house of
Caiaphas, Iscariot rejoined the apostles.
As yet they had no thought of his guilt.
But Jesus knew it as soon as he saw the
traitor's face, for Jesus could read men's
hearts. Yet Judas took his place with the

other eleven. On the following evening, when Jesus disclosed his knowledge that one whom he had chosen for close friend should betray him, the voice of Judas was heard with the others in protest, and " Is it I ? " he said. What dramatist could have devised that scene ? Or who could portray the look that passed when Jesus in the guise of a slave, passing from one apostle to another, presently knelt before Judas and washed his feet ?

On the earlier days of the week Jesus and the twelve doubtless had eaten their evening meal in Gethsemane after their return from the Temple. But on the Thursday they were to eat the more elaborate Passover supper, with its careful ceremonial, which could scarcely be done out-of-doors. Therefore they met in the large room which Jesus had arranged to borrow from a friend in Jerusalem. That friend and his family took their Paschal meal in another room, for Jesus would have none but the twelve with him. He had yet many things to say to them, and he knew that his death was near. He foresaw the utter despair that this would bring to his friends. Therefore, with astounding self-forgetfulness, he spent himself in preparing them for what was to come. More fully than ever he revealed himself to them, he tried to give them peace of mind, and strength, and faith, and a joy no outward disaster could take away. Once only did he reveal in the upper room his own inward agony and suspense as he thought of what was to come, when " That thou doest, do quickly ! " he said to the traitor. And Judas rose from his place, and went out to seek the chief priests.

If only by his death, as he was sure, could the Kingdom of God be established, Jesus would meet torture and death with an unmatched fortitude. Yet, though his enemies might do their worst, one thing he could not endure, and that was to be forgotten by his friends. Therefore on

P

this evening he bequeathed to them a rite by which those who loved him, then and after, should be united with one another and with him. The doctrines concerning it over which men differ are not to be discussed here. Enough to emphasize a truth concerning which all can agree. Whatever the richness of the gifts it bestows, it is not for our own sakes chiefly that we celebrate this rite. The ultimate reason is that by so doing we fulfil the bidding given in the upper room, and still, in every variety of setting, the bread is broken and the wine is poured because Jesus said " Do this in remembrance of me."

When all was finished, and the psalms appointed to end the Paschal meal had been sung, Jesus and the eleven left Jerusalem and made their way towards Gethsemane. As they walked, he told the disciples, amid their indignant protests, that soon they would repudiate him and think only of their own safety. Perhaps the tranquil certainty with which he said this hurt them more than any rebuke could have done, as afterwards their remorse must have been greater because he had said no word of blame.

They entered the orchard. Eight of the disciples lay down to sleep at their accustomed place. Peter, James, and John went further with Jesus, because he asked them to keep watch while he prayed. He knew that Iscariot had gone to the priests and would lead them to Gethsemane. He wished to be warned of their approach, not that he might fly—had he sought escape, he would not have gone to the usual place, where the traitor would rely upon finding him—but rather that he might end his prayers and advance to meet them.

Then Jesus bowed himself to the ground in an agony of soul. " O my Father, if it be possible, let this cup pass away from me ! " Jesus had revealed God as the Father of all men, yet made it plain that he held his own filial relationship to be essentially different from any to which even the disciples could attain. He assumed always as an evident fact that he was " the Son " in a unique sense. We have no true portrait of him if we omit that. " All things," he said, " have been delivered unto me of my Father : and no one knoweth the Son, save the Father; neither doth any know the Father, save the Son, and he to whomsoever the Son willeth to reveal Him." [1] The whole purpose of his life was to accomplish the Father's will, and that will was the setting up on earth of the kingdom of God. Of late he had become certain that his dying was the only way by which this could be brought about, and thus the Father's will done. But was there any other way, he asked again, as the awful horror of it closed in upon him? He

---

[1] It may be noted that it is not from the Fourth Gospel, but from two of the Synoptists, that we have these words.

prayed that, if so, it might be revealed.
Yet always, and before all else, he prayed
that he might do the Father's will.

As they listened, the three disciples,
spent with fatigue and emotion, fell asleep.
Presently he roused them, but had scarcely
turned to pray again before their eyes
closed. This happened once more. Then,
he said, they might sleep if they could.
The hour when vigilance might have served
him was past. The betrayer was within
the gate. Together let them meet him.
Judas advanced, with the priests, their
allies, and a contingent of the Temple
guard behind. The arranged signal was
given. It was the custom for a pupil to
salute a rabbi by a ceremonial kiss. Iscariot came to Jesus, and said, " Hail,
rabbi ! " and kissed him.

" My teacher ! " On that word Jesus
was led to death. When next would he
hear it ? Again in a garden, but at dawn,
not at night, from lips not treacherous but

passionately loyal, from an amazed, adoring woman who too would cry " My teacher ! " as she knew him.

VI

There can be no need to re-tell at length the story of the trials and crucifixion. It is set out in the Gospels with a simplicity, directness, and restraint upon which not the finest of literary craftsmen could improve. There are few points in it needing explanation. But we shall follow the sequence of events more readily if we bear in mind that there were two trials, ecclesiastical and civil, in each of which there were three stages. First, immediately after his arrest, Jesus was taken to the house of Annas, a former high-priest who had been deposed by the intervention of the Roman government. There followed his arraignment before the " council," or Sanhedrin, under the presidency of the high-priest,

Caiaphas. He was charged with having spoken blasphemy. Yet those who combined the parts of judges and accusers found a difficulty in obtaining any evidence. Their witnesses could not even fabricate a colourable and consistent story. But at last, in reply to Caiaphas, Jesus unhesitatingly claimed to be the divine Messiah. Thereupon, as tradition enjoined when blasphemy had been spoken, the high-priest "rent his clothes." There was no further need to trouble about witnesses, he said. They themselves had heard the prisoner blaspheme; what was their verdict? It was that he deserved death.

The third and final stage of the ecclesiastical trial had perforce to be delayed for an hour or two. According to the Law, these proceedings had been irregular, as the Sanhedrin could not hold a formal meeting except between dawn and sunset. Until the day broke, therefore, Jesus was exposed to the savagery of the mob. Then, in a few minutes, the formal session began and ended. The capital sentence was passed.

But the power of carrying it out had been taken from the Jewish authorities by the Romans. Therefore a civil trial had to follow, and Jesus was hurried off to the procurator. Here two new counts were added to the indictment. Pilate viewed the Jews and their religion with contempt. He would not easily be persuaded to reckon " blasphemy " as a crime justifying sentence of death. But " stirring up the people " and " forbidding to give tribute to Cæsar," of which also Jesus now stood accused, were in a very different category. Pilate knew, and the Jews knew that he knew, how short would be that procurator's tenure of office who spared any prisoner guilty of stirring disaffection against Rome.

Despite this knowledge, Pilate tried again and again to release Jesus. When he had interrogated the prisoner privately, he was wholly sure that the charges brought against him were due to mere malevolence. But the enemies of Jesus had filled the Prætorium with their hirelings. Pilate's sojourn in Palestine had not taught him much of a frenzied Oriental mob if he supposed that he could divert it from its prey by an appeal to justice or compassion. Then, after the first stage of the trial, Pilate, wishing to evade responsibility, sent this Galilæan prisoner to the tetrarch of Galilee, who was in Jerusalem for the Passover. Herod Antipas took this as a welcome compliment. But all his questions to the prisoner were met with an impenetrable silence, and Jesus, after being mocked and maltreated by Herod's troops, was sent back under escort to Pilate.

Once more that unhappy procurator tried to escape from what he knew would be at least a sacrifice of Roman justice to a corrupt and bloodthirsty mob. He would have tried yet more had not the fiendish ingenuity of their instigators put into the mouths of the people the one argument that could break Pilate's resistance. " If thou let this man go, thou art not Cæsar's friend ! " " Shall I crucify your king ? " " We have no king but Cæsar ! " Let him ignore that cry, and Pilate's own days were numbered. That the chief priests and their accomplices had suborned the very dregs of the city to achieve their end is made certain by those words to Pilate. To any patriotic and religious-minded Jew the idea that some of his fellow-countrymen, standing in Jerusalem itself, gathered at the very time of the Passover, should declare " We have no king but Cæsar ! " would have seemed revolting and incredible.

So the third and last stage of the trial ended. Pilate, who had tried to shift his responsibility to Herod, tried now to shift it to the crowd. Solemnly he washed his hands before them all. But it was he and no other who handed over Jesus to be crucified. Only when, presuming on their triumph, the high-priests bade him alter the inscription he had set upon the cross, did the true quality of his race re-assert itself. "What I have written, I have written," he answered, and in that curt reply rings the spirit of imperial Rome.

VII

There are some of us who cannot bear to dwell, as certain writers have brought themselves to do, upon all the horrible barbarities and indignities which Jesus had to suffer. Enough to remember that, in a sense, the very cruelty of his torturers overreached itself. As a rule, the victims of crucifixion lingered in agony for two or three days. But to Jesus, worn out already by exhaustion, and buffeting, and scourging, release came within some five hours—a space so unusually short that the soldiers wondered to find him already dead.

As he hung on the cross, Jesus the teacher

still taught, alike by his words and his silence. In his recorded words are a profound revelation of himself, for he prayed for his murderers, comforted a penitent thief, provided for his mother and a disciple, or ever he said a word of his own sufferings of soul and body. He taught by his silence also, for there was not a word of bitterness or reproach, and not one of regret for things done wrong or opportunities misused. He alone had no cause for sorrow as he looked back over his life; he alone could feel that he had left nothing undone, and could say of his every task, " It is finished ! "

When the moment came for Jesus to die, his last word, a sentence from a psalm, was so spoken that it gained for him a convert. Some power more than human seemed to reinforce him. For it was not in the faint whisper of the dying, but " with a loud voice " that he cried : " Father, into thy hands I commend my spirit ! " Near him stood a Roman officer, in charge of the soldiers guarding the place of execution. Through the hours he must have watched and listened with increasing wonder. And now, " when the centurion, which stood by over against him, saw that he so gave up the ghost, he said, Truly this man was the Son of God!"

Dare any say that he was wrong?

CHAPTER VIII

THE END—AND THE BEGINNING

I

CHRISTIANITY, which means belief in
Jesus as the divine Christ, the Son of God,
died on Good Friday.

These pages have attempted to show the
setting in which Jesus lived on earth, the
successive stages of his ministry, and the
varying opinions formed of him by his
contemporaries. We have noted that the
disciples when they joined him certainly did
not regard him as more than an attractive
rabbi. They did not become disciples
because they believed him divine; gradually
they came to believe him divine because
they had become disciples. In other words,
their belief was the result of their daily

experiences. As they listened to his words and lived in his company, they realized quickly that this rabbi was unlike any other rabbi. By degrees that conviction deepened into another—that this man stood apart from all other men. To that in turn succeeded what was at first a wild surmise, then a possibility, and then a certainty—" Thou art the Christ, the Son of the living God ! " Yet this newly-kindled faith flickered when Jesus spoke of his approaching death. It leapt up again on Palm Sunday. Then on Good Friday it died. All they had heard about a " rising again " seemed meaningless. Hope and faith were buried in the tomb. Only love and bitter sorrow remained. Christianity was dead.

Then something happened which caused it to rise from the dead. Something happened which was to transform men and women, which changed all existence for them, which gave them, after a few days of amazed and incredulous joy, a serene and enduring certainty. This new faith was not one of transient emotion; not one, again, to be limited to even a few millions of a single race. Beginning among the Jews of Palestine, it was to spread and conquer Europe. When the Roman Empire fell, Christianity did not fall with it. After nineteen centuries, it is still a supreme force in the world.

Christianity, which died on Good Friday, rose again from the dead. That is indisputable. Something must have happened to cause this. That also is beyond question. What was that something?

The New Testament offers an answer. It explains the resurrection of Christianity by affirming the Resurrection of Jesus Christ. That is an adequate cause. If we reject it, we must find some other adequate cause to replace it. Where can we find one? That these Galilæan peasants had either the power or the will to devise a colossal fraud, and endured martyrdom in order to maintain it, is inconceivable. Impostors neither live as the followers of Jesus Christ lived nor die as they died. That they were the victims of an illusion becomes almost as incredible, when we examine the evidence. The Gospels do not show us men confident that Jesus will rise again on the third day, and eagerly expecting his return. They show us men absolutely sure that they will never see their vanished master again in this world. They show us men who, on receiving the first news of the Resurrection, dismiss it impatiently as an idle tale. They show us men yielding to the evidence of facts slowly and—from fear lest they should be mistaken—reluctantly.

Are we to suppose that the Resurrection story was a pious legend, the accretion of a later age, which found its way into the creed of the Church? Unhappily for such a theory, the Church itself was based upon absolute certainty of the Resurrection.

Q

Instead of returning dejectedly to their
homes, the disciples remained together in
Jerusalem because their risen master had
so bidden them, and because their immediate work was to bear witness of
his Resurrection to the world. Moreover,
legends are of slow growth. They are not
universally accepted within the lifetime of
those who can contradict them. Here,
again, the historical evidence is decisive.
We turn to St. Paul's first Corinthian letter.
It was written twenty-six years only after
the Crucifixion. St. Paul insists that belief
in the resurrection of man—concerning
which some of his friends at Corinth were
doubtful—must follow upon belief in the
Resurrection of Jesus, which none of them
doubted. He himself has tested the evidence again, has made a list of those occasions
when the risen Lord appeared. Among
them he mentions an appearance to " about
five hundred brethren at once," the greater
part of whom, he adds, are still alive. Five

hundred men at once could scarcely be deceived by an illusion. Also it is obvious that St. Paul knows many of the survivors who claimed to have seen the risen Jesus, and has questioned them and compared their accounts.

II

Many devout persons, while firmly holding as truth that Jesus rose from death, have tried to make the Resurrection easier to believe by a " spiritualized " interpretation. They would say that the body did not rise, but that Jesus manifested himself in some psychical way to the consciousness of his disciples, so that they might be sure of his having triumphed over death. Such theories have been given many different forms, each of which is apt to raise difficulties more serious than those it is designed to remove. But two things may be said of them all. The first is that, whatever their intrinsic probability or improbability, they do not represent what the disciples believed, what St. Paul believed, or what the early Church believed. Of course this is not conclusive in itself; the disciples and the five hundred brethren may have been mistaken. Yet, beyond any question, what they believed, and the Church through them, was that on the third day the spirit of Jesus returned to the body in the tomb, that his resurrected body, transfigured and endowed with new supernatural powers as it was, was one with that body which had hung on the cross and been wounded by nails and spear. And thus he came forth from the tomb and made himself known when he would to his friends.

The other point to be observed in attempts to explain away the bodily resurrection of Jesus is that they spring from a fixed dislike of the supernatural, and a conviction that the Gospels will be more widely credited in proportion as the supernatural element can be eliminated from their narratives. Yet in a Christian that seems to betray confused thinking. " Whom say ye that I am? " We must return, after all, to that fundamental question. Jesus claimed to be the divine Son of God. We have seen how that claim is inherent in all his teaching. We have seen that his question cannot be evaded by a pretence of distinguishing between the teaching and the claims of him who gave it. If those claims were untrue, then he was either a deluded fanatic, suffering from an arrogance and egotism akin to mania, or an impostor. If he is not worthy of our worship, he is not worthy of our love. Studying again the story of his life, the perfect character set forth in the Gospels, the teaching given by word, and deed, and character, we feel that Jesus is what he claimed to be. But when we admit that when we accept Jesus as the Son of God, difficulties about the " supernatural " are at an end. They have no longer the slightest cogency. For him, indeed, the supernatural is natural. Because Jesus was the Son of God, we should expect him to rise from the dead. Because he was the Son of God, we should expect the manner of his rising to transcend human experience. We should have far more reason to be sceptical if it did not.

The same considerations will apply to the story of the Virgin Birth. Of set purpose, nothing was said of that in the first pages of this book, because our view of it will depend far less upon its place in Christian literature and tradition than upon our answer to " Whom say ye that I am ? " when we have completed our study of his life and character. Of course the two events do not stand on the same plane of importance, and the historical evidence for the Resurrection is far stronger than that for the Virgin Birth. Yet it is from the other point of view that we best approach the question. Were the claims of Jesus false? Then the Virgin Birth goes, with the Resurrection and all else. Were they true? Then the birth of the Son of God was itself the supreme miracle, apart altogether from its manner. And that the Son of God should be born otherwise than merely human beings is not strange; the supernatural, once more, seems natural.

III

We return to the stories of the Resurrection. There are inconsistencies of detail between them, and they would be less credible if there were none. For these are no fabrications, carefully planned to harmonize and confirm one another at every point. These are memories of actual things seen and heard in a time of extreme bewilderment and emotion. How easily the memory may slip on points of detail under such a strain is well known. We need

go back no further than to accounts of the
Great War for instances. When different
people describe a battle of no more than
ten years ago, they are likely enough to be
at variance about the position of a unit, the
hour when a message was received or an
advance ordered, even though each writes
from experience, and each is convinced of
his accuracy. Who can wonder that there
are discrepancies over time and place in
the various records of the Resurrection?

They do not matter. What does matter
is the convincing truthfulness of the stories
as a whole. They are told so artlessly, yet
with little touches of human nature that
no deviser of imagined tales could have
supplied. What writer inventing appear-
ances of the Lord rising triumphant from
the grave would have made him show
himself first, not to a worshipping crowd,
not to his apostles, but to Mary Magdalene?
Or let any read with an alert literary sense
the one story of an appearance which is

told at any length by the Synoptists—
St. Luke's account of the journey to
Emmaus. Assuredly he will feel that every
syllable of it rings true. He will note how
graphic and true to life it is, even in its
incidental touches : Cleophas's comment,
blunt almost to discourtesy, " Surely you
must be the only man in Jerusalem, even
among its temporary residents, who has not
heard of what has happened there in these
last few days ! " Or, again, the frank
despair of " We hoped that it was he which
should redeem Israel "—" we hoped, but
we have had to abandon that hope."
Through this, as through all the Resurrection stories, we are made to feel the
perfect serenity, the forgiving love, that
now flow from the risen Jesus to his friends.

Then the day came when his visible
presence must be withdrawn. Again, why
should we doubt the simple record of its
manner ? Jesus was not come to teach his
disciples physics or astronomy. He chose

a way that would make it easy for these children to know that he had left the world and gone unto the Father. His last words were a benediction, and, while he still blessed, a cloud received him out of their sight.

And they, who lately had fled headlong from Gethsemane at the first sign of danger, now returned to Jerusalem, the one place of extreme peril for them, " with great joy."

IV

It was an end. But it was also a beginning. When St. Luke prefaced the Acts, he referred to his earlier Gospel as a record of what " Jesus began both to do and to teach." The word is just. The work begun in those three years was to be continued through every age, and in each the promise of his unseen Presence is fulfilled. The final worth of the Gospels is to put before us not the mere biography of a departed saint, but the portrait of a living Person.

"Whom say ye that I am?" Each of us must make his answer. We are free, if we will, to deny his claims, to reject his appeal for our love. Yet we might well prefer to be mistaken with St. John than to be right with Herod and Iscariot—if the claims were false.

But they are not false. The Jesus who lived and died is the Jesus who lives; the same yesterday, and to-day, and for ever.

RABBONI

A STUDY OF JESUS CHRIST THE TEACHER

By CANON ANTHONY C. DEANE, M.A.

6/- net

Sir W. Robertson Nicoll in *The British Weekly*.

"In this book he sets himself a definite task; he endeavours to detach and bring out in relief the figure of our Lord as the supreme Teacher. Such a detached study has real value and importance. . . . Canon Deane has carried out his aim with singular success. His chapters and paragraphs move on in masterly sequence. The style is lucid, forcible and felicitous, lit up with brilliant epigrams. . . . The book represents clarified and condensed thinking of no common order. Even though you may hesitate to adopt all its positions, you are constrained to admire the sweet and reverent spirit, the deep-hearted faith, which breathe throughout this ' Study of Jesus Christ as Teacher.' . . . If we felt inclined to criticise the book as a whole, we should complain of its brevity. The author has planned and thought out his ' Study' with such scholarly care that it keeps a genuine unity and proportion. Within his self-imposed limits he says as much as could be said; but he says it so well that he will make his readers wish he had found room to say more."

The Methodist Recorder.

"I have done with Canon Deane's *Rabboni* what I have not done with any book for many a long day. After I had read it through, I turned back to the first page and read it through a second time, and then I went and bought another copy to bestow upon a friend. The Canon has many old things to say in an extremely fresh way, and many new things that he puts persuasively."

HODDER & STOUGHTON, Ltd., Publishers, London

OUR FATHER

A STUDY OF THE LORD'S PRAYER

By CANON ANTHONY C. DEANE, M.A.

3/6 net

The Student Movement.

"This beautiful little study of the Lord's Prayer is one of a series of 'Little Books on the Christian Life,' which should help to make the old faith live anew for modern readers. . . . Not only does the author shed new light upon the familiar petitions, one by one, but he shows us the Prayer as a work of art, a complete thing of beauty."

The Christian World.

"Canon Deane limits himself in this volume to the simple but profitable task of investigating afresh the structure of the Lord's Prayer, and re-examining its language with the aid of the fuller knowledge of New Testament Greek which has recently come to us. The result is that the whole prayer is lighted up, while several of the petitions —notably those for daily bread and for deliverance from temptation—take on a new and deeper meaning. The high quality of Canon Deane's work is well known, and this book, by reason of its devout tone, spiritual insight and practical helpfulness, should appeal to a wide circle of readers."

HODDER & STOUGHTON, LTD., PUBLISHERS, LONDON

HOW TO ENJOY THE BIBLE

(THE PEOPLE'S LIBRARY)

By CANON ANTHONY C. DEANE, M.A.

2/6 net

The Church Times.

"The little book is an introduction to the Bible in a true and literal sense. For it leads its reader into a field which may or may not be known in part to him, but which he will at least know better for Canon Deane's guidance. After he has mastered it he will find that there is a lifetime's opportunity before him of further exploration, in the fields of exegesis and, perhaps, of mystical interpretation. Canon Deane has given us many scholarly and serviceable books, but none, we think, that will leave more readers his grateful debtor."

The Daily Telegraph.

"It is a book of immense value and will be gratefully read by many."

The Manchester Guardian.

"A book for everyone is Canon Anthony Deane's *How to Enjoy the Bible.* I have tested it by what always seems to me the true test of the usefulness of such a book—namely, by the extent to which it sends the reader from itself to the Bible it treats of—and it passes the test well. Those who read it will want to read their Bible more."

HODDER & STOUGHTON, LTD., PUBLISHERS, LONDON

New Titles.

A Boys and Girls Life of Christ.
         by Archd. J. Paterson-Smyth.

Everyman's Life of Jesus
         by the Rev. Prof. James Moffatt

Bonnet and Shawl.
         by Philip Guedalla

Slavery
         by Lady Simon.

The Story of My Life.
         by Helen Keller.

ORDER FORM for
Hodder & Stoughton's
People's Library

2/6
net each
Volume

..........The Beginnings of Man. By Edwin Oliver James

..........My Religion. By Helen Keller

..........New Silent Friends. By Richard King

..........The Return Journey. By Richard King

..........One Quiet Evening. By Richard King

..........How to Enjoy Health.
By Claude Lillingston and Norah Hill

..........Making of Man. By Sir Oliver Lodge

..........Ether and Reality. By Sir Oliver Lodge

..........Evolution and Creation. By Sir Oliver Lodge

..........Dr. Johnson and Company. By Robert Lynd

..........Coal and Its Story. By E. A. Martin

..........Arthur Mee's People's Bible

....X...The Middle Ages. By E. B. Osborn

..........Socrates and His Friends. By E. B. Osborn

..........Our Debt to Greece and Rome. By E. B. Osborn

..........Some Things That Matter. By Lord Riddell

..........More Things That Matter. By Lord Riddell

..........The Poetry of Architecture. By Frank Rutter

..........The Old Masters. By Frank Rutter

..........Nerves in Disorder. By Dr. A. T. Schofield

..........A People's Life of Christ
By Archdeacon J. Paterson-Smyth

..........The Gospel of the Hereafter.
By Archdeacon J. Paterson-Smyth

..........Atoms and Electrons. By J. W. N. Sullivan

..........Everyday Biology. By Professor J. Arthur Thomson

..........The Control of the Mind. By Robert H. Thouless

..........John Bunyan. By The Dean of Winchester
By Marcus Woodward

..........How to Enjoy Wild Flowers. By Marcus Woodward

..........How to Enjoy Garden Flowers
By Marcus Woodward

..........How to Enjoy the Starry Sky. By Marcus Woodward

..........How to Enjoy Birds. By Marcus Woodward

Name..

Address...

HODDER AND STOUGHTON